# All the Classroom's a Stage

# All the Classroom's a Stage

## *Applying Theater Principles to Teaching Techniques*

Michael Flanagan
Rose Burnett Bonczek

ROWMAN & LITTLEFIELD
Lanham • Boulder • New York • London

Published by Rowman & Littlefield
An imprint of The Rowman & Littlefield Publishing Group, Inc.
4501 Forbes Boulevard, Suite 200, Lanham, Maryland 20706
www.rowman.com

6 Tinworth Street, London SE11 5AL, United Kingdom

Copyright © 2020 by Michael Flanagan and Rose Burnett Bonczek

*All rights reserved.* No part of this book may be reproduced in any form or by any electronic or mechanical means, including information storage and retrieval systems, without written permission from the publisher, except by a reviewer who may quote passages in a review.

British Library Cataloguing in Publication Information Available

Library of Congress Control Number: 2020945796
ISBN 978-1-4758-5367-4 (cloth)
ISBN 978-1-4758-5368-1 (pbk.)
ISBN 978-1-4758-5369-8 (electronic)

Mike: To Melanie, for the best adventure

Rose: To my mother, a scholar of storytelling and my first teacher

# Contents

| | | |
|---|---|---|
| Preface | | ix |
| Acknowledgments | | xv |
| Introduction: Us vs. Them: Dawn of Something Better | | xvii |
| 1 | Theatrical Concepts Applied to the Classroom | 1 |
| 2 | The Teacher as Performance Artist | 11 |
| 3 | Creating the Story | 33 |
| 4 | All of Your Classroom *Is* a Stage | 49 |
| 5 | Your Students as Your Acting Partners | 63 |
| 6 | The Educator as Director | 83 |
| 7 | Your Stage in Action: Using Theater to Teach Writing | 101 |
| Conclusion: The Curtain Call | | 117 |
| Appendix A: Blind Offers (via Keith Johnstone in *Impro*) | | 119 |
| Appendix B: Come Join Me (via Viola Spolin) | | 121 |
| Appendix C: Dinner Party | | 125 |
| Appendix D: Explosion Tag | | 129 |
| Appendix E: Freeze Tag | | 133 |
| Appendix F: Kitty Wants a Corner | | 137 |
| Appendix G: Observe 6 | | 141 |
| Appendix H: One-Word-at-a-Time Storytelling | | 145 |

| | |
|---|---:|
| Appendix I: Simultaneous Clap | 149 |
| Appendix J: Three-Headed Alien | 151 |
| Appendix K: Walk and Rename Objects (Keith Johnstone) | 153 |
| Appendix L: What Are You Doing? | 157 |
| Appendix M: Zing | 161 |
| Appendix N: Physical Exercise: Home Rehearsal for Teachers | 165 |
| Appendix O: Laban Movement Analysis | 169 |
| Appendix P: Vocal Warm Up | 171 |
| Appendix Q: The Uta Hagen Nine Questions | 177 |
| Appendix R: Exercises for Ice Breakers, Getting Acquainted | 179 |
| Appendix S: Exercises to Strengthen Collaborative Skills | 181 |
| Appendix T: Exercises to Develop Imagination and Empowerment | 183 |
| Appendix U: Exercises to Strengthen Focus, Awareness, and Observation | 185 |
| Appendix V: Exercises to Strengthen Listening and Being Present | 187 |
| Appendix W: Exercises to Physically Energize | 189 |
| Bibliography | 191 |
| Index | 193 |
| About the Authors | 201 |

# Preface

A hearty welcome to this workshop—well, work*book*—that we created to support you and your teaching. We offer skills, stories, exercises, and ideas you can bring to your practice, classroom, and students. We are theater practitioners and college professors with a combined forty-five years of experience between us, and we arrived at these methods after much experimentation, trial, and success in our classrooms and rehearsal studios. We've learned through the years that the core skills that a theater practitioner needs are remarkably similar to those of a teacher, and the more we applied theater to our teaching, the more dynamic and grounded our teaching became.

There's no great mystery to understanding theater concepts, because theater skills are *human* skills. Even if the word "drama" struck fear in your heart in the past, you've certainly listened to, connected with, and collaborated with others, and have been present in a moment. That's it. Those are the skills at the core of performance. Knowing how actors or directors develop and strengthen those skills can positively affect your craft of teaching, regardless of your subject. You don't need to have taken a theater class, or performed in any plays, to benefit from the information and guidance we offer here.

## MIKE

In one of the first classes I taught—English Literature—the chair of the department observed me teaching *A Midsummer Night's Dream*. The non-English-major students were required to take the course. Yet the chair saw excited students on their feet, acting out scenes and playing with ideas, and taking wild but accurate stabs at interpreting Shakespeare's language.

Afterward, the chair asked me, "How'd you get them all so involved?" Before I could answer, he said, "I guess sometimes you just get a good group." I thought about how quiet and uninterested they'd been for the first weeks, and how I'd brought techniques I'd learned as a theater director into the classroom. Whether we were reading a play or a five-hundred-year-old poem, I got them on their feet, used theater concepts that encouraged them to connect with the material, and applied everything I knew about directing, acting, and improvisation to teach that class.

Over the years, I applied the same techniques to classes a lot of my colleagues dreaded teaching: core writing classes; study skills and college orientation; and speech, debate, and career communication. All the students in those classes engaged and connected with me, with one another, and with the curriculum.

Students finished with stronger grades, with a positive opinion of higher education, and with far more abilities in their later classes and, eventually, their careers. The approach and techniques I used in acting classes, in workshops, and in directing theater productions worked in every classroom I entered. Because theater, as it turns out, is teaching and learning.

## ROSE

I'd been a theater director, actor, and deviser for years before I stepped into my first college classroom to teach, and it was love at first sight. It felt like coming home, because I realized that I'd already been teaching in my theater work throughout my whole life. Creating, directing, and performing plays prepared me for a collaborative give-and-take in the classroom that made the learning process with my students dynamic, creative, productive, and *fun*.

I assumed this was how everyone taught, whether theater or science or psychology. Later, when I began to mentor graduate students with teaching fellowships, I found this wasn't the case. One of the most frequent concerns they shared was, "I learn so much about protocols and theory; how do I get better at *doing* it? *How* do I communicate and engage with students on my feet?" What I heard them saying was, "How do I become a better *performer* as a teacher?" Those who had pursued acting and theater first, though, unanimously said, "Thank goodness for my theater training. Otherwise I wouldn't have known what the heck to do once I got in front of a class."

I started to offer workshops to new adjuncts and grad students in our department on how to intentionally apply collaboration and ensemble building techniques to the craft of teaching. We worked on empathy, listening, trust, and applying the essential acting skills of awareness, focus, and being present to teaching. Soon, I was asked to do workshops for new faculty and nontheater teachers at the Center for Teaching. I thought, *Hmmm. What would happen if I didn't change any of the theater exercises in this workshop? Let's roll the dice and see.*

What happened was thrilling; the teachers I worked with, from all areas of expertise, immediately understood these theater exercises—mainly because they were framed in the world of play. Well, by starting to play again in those workshops, faculty members made some pretty serious discoveries about teaching: how we could be more empathetic and better connect with our students and ourselves, and inject new sources of inspiration into our craft.

## WHY IT WORKS

At the core of every great piece of theater is a good story. Theater artists—actors and directors—are expert storytellers. If you can tell a good story about a human moment that people recognize and relate to, they will be touched, inspired, and changed by that experience.

We'd like to tell you a story.

Imagine if you will: At a recent faculty meeting the dean paused to discuss the ways we teachers might better engage students. We were shocked at the possibility that the meeting might veer into territory directly connected to the student experience: teaching techniques, and maybe addressing much-needed resources—potentially leaving behind, even for a glorious instant, the constant litany of accreditation and regulatory requirements. So we dropped our pens and lifted our chins.

She said she'd been walking down the halls and looking in classrooms and was disappointed to discover many teachers sitting at their desks, having class discussions or giving lectures from a relaxed, seated position.

Her solution? "Why don't you walk up and down the aisles while you teach?"

Our collective eyebrows raised.

"You know. Walk to the back of the room. Teach from back there. It'll throw them off. Keep them listening. Then walk to the front again."

Walk to the back? Throw them off?

Over the last few years, too many of our students—at an alarming rate—have been turning away from the discussions, lectures, and assignments of the classroom and finding greater interest in text messages, sports recaps, and protestations from YouTube stars, all shining like a welcoming beacon from cell phones hidden on their laps. They have trouble keeping track of their assignments, accurately doing those assignments, and for some, bothering to do them at all. They wander in late, or leave early, or don't show up at all.

We had tried everything: we abandoned the lecture, played music, clarified instructions, simplified assignments, created bigger consequences for lateness, eliminated consequences for lateness, adjusted our lessons, and tried not to stay on one idea or subject for too long for fear that those eyes would glaze over, turn away, and go into the light—only to receive the collective, unwelcome student response of complete, abject apathy.

In this particular faculty meeting, we'd just been given a . . . solution? "Walk to the back of the room. Teach from back there."

Before the dean had even finished her explanation of how such a maneuver would correct our twenty-first-century pedagogical ails, most of us had checked out. The problem of student engagement wasn't our position in the classroom, where we sat or stood, walked, or didn't walk.

The only effect this would have would be to adjust our angle of observation. From the front, we could see the students staring at their barely hidden cell phones, or maybe at the tabletop, or sometimes even in our general direction, eyes glazed, pen rolling between their fingers, their thoughts far from thesis statements or calculating sine curves or identifying chemical compounds.

From the back of the room? Same students, different angle.

So often a Band-Aid is offered by someone who then deftly avoids a deeper examination of the patient. Walking back and forth might offer a good stretch of the legs, but it doesn't offer much else—and why would you want to "throw off" a student anyway? That very statement feeds into an old notion of something adversarial between teacher and student—as if somehow we didn't share the same goals.

Sometimes, no matter how prepared we are, the traditional view of the space—"here's my spot, that's yours; let's not cross the line"—can defeat us long before we walk into the room on that first, hopeful day of class. Separation runs so much deeper than the expected division in the physical space of a classroom.

The solution needed to be bigger. More impactful. More . . . *essential*. Like a good story. And in the classroom—the performance space you share with your student collaborators—we found theatrical storytelling provided that solution.

## WHY NOW?

Why this book at this moment in time? Actually, this book has been needed for a while, but in the changing world of education and the rapid advent of technology in our lives and the lives of our students, that need has become even more critical. Why are enrollment and retention rates dropping (in some cases, precipitously)? Why do so many students struggle to pay attention in class? Why are so many students—despite your best efforts—ill prepared for their future prospects when they reach graduation?

By using theater concepts as a model, these vital issues can be addressed. Using this workbook as a guide, you'll gain valuable insights into your unique teaching methods, with straightforward recommendations on how to enhance your craft to more effectively—and playfully—reach and teach your students.

It begins with a change in our understanding of the classroom itself. Instead of the old teaching concept of "sage on the stage," we believe the whole classroom is the stage. Through theatrical collaboration and storytelling, you and your students will create this stage *together*.

We finished writing this book before the COVID-19 pandemic caused a major change at most educational institutions: the shift to primarily online learning. We know this shift will be short-lived, and after reading this book, we're confident you'll be able to apply the concepts and exercises in any classroom, regardless of subject-matter, and in-person, hybrid, or online. For a sample of online applications of these ideas, go to: http://roseburnettbonczek.com/.

# Acknowledgments

We are very thankful to our "early readers." As we discuss in this book, the process of writing can very quickly lead you into a forest you can't see for the trees. We've been very lucky to have a group of excellent shamans, spirit guides, Gandalfs, and Obi-Wans. Without their time and incredibly hard work, this book—and we—wouldn't have made it. For all the notes, suggestions, edits, discoveries, ideas, and research, thank you to Ally Callaghan, Valerie Clayman Pye, Melanie Flanagan, Katie Greaves, Helen Huff, Steve Kaliski, Noel MacDuffie, Kate McGraw, Barbara Morganfield, and Lucie Rossi. Their cheerful willingness to read (and reread!) early chapters gave us new ideas, fresh perspective, and inspiration.

We're so grateful to Christian De Matteo for the invaluable insight into not only the content but also the writing and structure, and for his sense of humor, excitement about the project, and constant encouragement.

Thanks to the teachers and teaching artists whose conversations were invaluable to the content. So much of this book is about the teaching experience, and these great educators helped expand not only our approach but also our ideas and understanding of teaching. Thank you to Lisa Jill Anderson, Tom Carrozza, Sabrina Cataudella, Joseph DiTargiani, Amy Hughes, Roger Manix, Joe McGraw, Jay Nickerson, Damon Noland, Julie Orkis, Alexandra Slater, David Storck, Laura Tesman, Jolie Tong, and Ian Wen.

Thanks to Sarah Jubar for her initial inspiration and support of the book; to Emily Tuttle, assistant editor, and Carlie Wall, managing editor, at Rowman & Littlefield, Lauren Davis, senior editor, and Laura Hussey, theater and performance editor at Routledge Press, for their early encouragement; to Tom Koerner, editorial director at Rowman & Littlefield, and Megan DeLancey, associate production editor, for shepherding this project to the finish line; and to all the editors at Rowman & Littlefield Publishers.

# Introduction

## Us vs. Them: Dawn of Something Better

### US VS. THEM

Much of the educational system encourages division via competition and separation. "I got a better grade than yours. I work harder than you, speak more often in class than you, and study longer than you. My honors class is better than your nonhonors class." For teachers, the dividing line extends within us as well; often it's simply the difference between how we'd *like* to teach a class and how we *have* to teach it.

The enormous number of constantly changing regulations has divided and separated many of us from our connection to our areas of expertise and our interest in creatively delivering information, and most of all, it has disconnected us from our love for our subject. Exhaustion at being overworked, lowered morale in response to budget cuts and denied resources, and lower pay rates have separated teachers from their creative energy, enthusiasm, and engagement, creating a dividing line between teachers and their ability to bring their unique strengths to the classroom.

So what can help erase this division and offer much-needed support for teachers stranded on the front lines?

### Theater

Theater is the opposite of division, of the Us vs. Them mentality that contributes to so many of the challenges in and out of the classroom. The nature of theater in its ideal form is one of erasing dividing lines. Its very purpose is to bring people together in a shared space to listen, learn, illuminate, and educate.

Unique, passionate artists come together to *collaborate* on a story. Whether writing, acting, directing, or designing, these artists have very specific goals—to write a play, perform a role, lead the ensemble, and create the physical world—void of any division and specifically for the purpose of telling a unified story. What if we could create a theatrical environment for our students and ourselves, coming together as actors, directors, and designers to tell a great story?

Story isn't that different from a classroom lesson, and the same skills and concepts that have been used to tell some of the world's most well known stories can be applied in the classroom. If we consider the entirety of our classroom as a stage—and we're all players and storytellers within that stage—then we take the first big steps toward creating "we" instead of Us vs. Them.

Our college students have always had challenges in their learning, and those have only increased over time. From poor school districts unable to afford the same level of college prep as the school in the wealthier district to the ubiquitous presence of social media and feel-good distractions that lead to impact on memory, retention, and focus, our students are trying to earn their college education in a rapid-fire changing world that—despite protestations—doesn't give everyone the same opportunities.

In recent years we've seen college admission scandals, greedy for-profit institutions that saddle unprepared students with horrific student loan debt, and instances where some schools can afford a college prep counselor, and some can't. Add to that an adherence to old methods and protocols that don't keep pace with or address our students' real-world experiences, and no wonder Us vs. Them has proliferated.

The good news is that there are indications of positive change in some corners, but there's nothing cohesive (yet) in broader policies to achieve consistency for reversing these trends. Adapting theater techniques and concepts in your classroom will create a collaborative and supportive environment that can counter some of those trends head-on. Through each chapter, we'll offer techniques in far greater detail, but these core ideas will help you create a lively, engaged, and enthusiastic class:

- Embrace yourself as a performer, and be able to examine the innate communication and intuitive skills you already possess so you can intentionally apply them to active performance in the classroom.
- Overcome any student-held beliefs that all classroom material is a boring, unhelpful, and unnecessary slog through a long and bothersome day. You'll teach a lesson *as a story*, drawing your students in through the story's nuances like a wise, trickster wizard.

- Erase the dividing line in the classroom and overcome the Us vs. Them mentality by turning it into a stage space, creatively shared by you and your students.
- Overcome any division between yourself and your students; since you can't get younger or set off an electromagnetic pulse that permanently destroys their cell phones, you need to find an acting partner in your students, like fellow storytellers performing a piece. Or you can become a director, shaping the world of the play in that classroom and encouraging all those collaborative artists to tell the story together.

The results of using theater techniques are far more essential to education: a more productive, engaged learning environment in which your students meet outcomes more successfully, improve their understanding of material, increase their grades, and begin to shape their learning into something they can apply going forward.

Collaborative learning creates room to bring back your original, dynamic vision of how you would like to teach the material, and it nurtures new love for material that's long since gone stale. Like the students you're guiding, you just need to start with a first step—not up and down the aisle but straight toward that shared space you're creating, a safe and supportive environment where you and your students will come together as acting partners, storytellers, and collaborators using theater techniques to create a meaningful educational experience.

*Chapter One*

# Theatrical Concepts Applied to the Classroom

### THEATER IS FUN — AND EFFECTIVE

For many, the word "theater" conjures the image of a few student plays at schools, a Broadway megahit, or some stereotypical acting games they've seen in comedies where someone pretends to be a tree. Sometimes it's viewed as being a mysterious and wondrous process, attainable by only a rarified few.

It isn't often that the first thought is, *This kind of collaborative play is serious business and has a vital contribution to education*, especially at the college level. The specific approaches and exercises that make theater a vital, collaborative art form can do the same for you, your craft of teaching, and your classroom environment.

How? Demystifying performance and acting for the nonpractitioner is essential to answer this question. When we watch a piece of theater, a guy stands on the stage and talks to another guy, and we, the audience, believe the story they're telling together. Or a woman stands on the stage alone and belts out a ballad accompanied by an orchestra, and we're moved by the story she tells.

It's a mystery to most audiences as to *how* that actor drew them into the story so deeply that they gasped when the guy revealed a secret. They don't know *how* that actress brought an unexpected lump to their throats when she sang about losing her love. They just know it happened, and those actor/magicians *made* it happen through the believability and truth they created onstage.

How does this connect to teaching? How could this connect to a classroom?

Without the help of these theater makers, many people would have left their ability to embrace and believe an imaginary story behind in their childhood. Those of us who chose theater as a career, however, sought ways to strengthen the skills that allowed us to be completely immersed in a story, as well as the skills to make someone else believe it.

To do that, we were taught a multitude of techniques, games, and ideologies that all tie into stripping away the real world and making the story of the play *our* world. These games and techniques strengthen important skills like listening, developing empathy, and connecting with others, which is accomplished through the collaborative play that theater making requires.

So, what initially may seem like a mysterious process is simply the result of many years of proficient training in—well—*play*. The benefits of play beyond the arts and sports have been well researched, and in recent years those benefits have been acknowledged and used in the worlds of business, science (actor Alan Alda teaches improvisation to scientists at the Alan Alda Center for Communicating Science at Stonybrook University), and most important, in education, child development, and learning. And doesn't everyone learn and strengthen their innate social skills through years of recess and unstructured play before they enter college?

Well, maybe not as much as they used to. As new technology became available, administrators, corporations, and educators were quick to provide computers, tablets, and software in the classroom, intensify training in technological skills, and increase the emphasis on academic and college readiness at younger ages. However, along with those good intentions to prepare children for the future came decisions to reduce recess time, limit or eliminate theater and music, and pare down any extracurricular activities that weren't viewed as supporting efforts to make our students more competitive in a quickly changing world (Reilly 2017).

The result? An absence of activities that include play and collaborative skills. Ironically, this has led to an *increase* in adolescent students who aren't equipped for a college-level education. Beckie Supiano, writing for the *Chronicle of Higher Education*, reports that "forty percent of students at four-year public colleges take at least one remedial class—for which they're paying college tuition, but not doing college-level work. Two-thirds of students at community colleges do. Whatever a high-school diploma signifies, it's not that a student is ready for first-year college classes" (Supiano 2013).

This decrease in college students' emotional and social readiness is cause for concern. In 2010, University of Michigan released a startling report that pointed to "a precipitous decline in the past 30 years in the percentage of college students who report having empathetic concern for others and who are willing to take on another person's perspective" (Hayden 2010). In addition, the report noted that over a ten-year period, college students' empathy levels dropped 40 percent (Szalavitz 2010).

Additional studies have rung the alarm even louder. According to Erika Christakis, an early childhood teacher and former preschool director, and Nicholas Christakis, a professor of medicine and sociology at Harvard University,

> When a four-year-old destroys someone's carefully constructed block castle or a 20-year-old belligerently monopolizes the class discussion on a routine basis, we might conclude that they are unaware of the feelings of the people around them. . . . The real "readiness" skills that make for an academically successful kindergartener or college student have as much to do with emotional intelligence as they do with academic preparation. Kindergartners need to know not just sight words and lower case letters, but how to search for meaning. The same is true of 18-year-olds.

According to Peter Gray, author of "The Decline of Play and the Rise of Psychopathology in Children and Adolescents," skills-based education without elements of play can also lead to "increased anxiety and depression," a "reduced sense of personal control," and "increased narcissism" (Gray 2011, 447–51). Theater play in the classroom, then, isn't an extracurricular addition; it's a necessity for teaching and learning.

Some of us, and some of our students, had the advantage of extensive playtime as children. We played tag, hide and seek, baseball, and basketball outside. Indoors, we played cards, Candyland, Monopoly, and Hungry Hungry Hippos. We created elaborate roles in stories of our own imaginations. "You be the crocodile, and I'll be the fish trying to escape; you be the evil witch who tries to freeze everyone, and I'll be the good witch who has the magic power to unfreeze the people."

When we got a little older, the messages changed: time to work, no time for play, play is for little kids, play is just for sports, and even then play *hard*, play to *win*; you don't want to be a loser; and if I catch you playing instead of working, there'll be trouble. And as for our imaginations? The message could be even harsher: get your head out of the clouds, come down to earth, stop daydreaming, and what are you, a weirdo? The message of play as a good and fun activity changed to that of play as childish and something to be outgrown.

The desire to play and to exercise our imagination is innate though, and introducing theater back into our lives can rekindle the positive benefits play can bring. However, if that innate desire is fighting against societal expectations, and no action is taken to reinforce the importance of play in school, then that creates fertile ground for fear to set in. This could be fear of being rejected and excluded, fear of failure, and most of all, fear of being judged by others. It can be pretty tough to reintroduce play and imagination as healthy pursuits in learning—and teaching—when fear is waiting there to cut us off from our potential.

## FEAR: THE GREAT DIVIDER

If we allow it, fear can govern much of a teacher's life. The stakes are high in education, whether they're the needs of a classroom full of students, the administration's new and sudden requirements, or our upcoming presentation at a national conference. And that little voice in our heads, stoking fears, is so, so loud.

What if I can't get this information across and the students don't do well? What if they're not prepared for the state exam and funding is cut? What if the administration is unhappy with the work I'm doing? What if my students think I'm a bad teacher or that I don't know what I'm talking about? What if I don't get tenure? What if I try this new theater thing and the students hate it?

Fear governs much of students' lives as well. Students fear failure: what if I fail this big test, paper, speech, or even the whole class? What if I raise my hand and give the answer and I'm wrong and look stupid in front of everyone? What if this class and degree is a waste of time and I'll never get a job and end up just like my parents?

That's a lot of fear. Fortunately, one of the most important benefits of theater as a form of play is it helps people conquer their fears. Theater prepares us to take risks and act on impulse without concerning ourselves with what people will think. It helps us let go of the potential negative possibilities of what could happen next—and instead, to act, to offer someone something they need, and to live in confidence that that person will respond in kind. Here we find one of the keys to conquering fear: taking the focus off the fear and putting it on the more important work of connecting with another person.

Regardless of their specialization, theater makers all learn how to collaborate, how to build the bonds of trust and mutual support, and in doing so, every group in each production has the potential to elevate the story because of the benefits of collaboration. Theater artists trust in their directors and scene partners, fellow designers, and other collaborators, and know that the trust is returned.

In learning theater skills tied to trust, support, and collaboration, we're reminded of what life was like when we were kids. As children, we not only created entire imaginary worlds but also developed the skills that would encourage and invite others to come and play with us in those worlds. The better we made the world, the more kids would want to join—and come back again and again.

# THE SKILLS AND METHODS OF THE ACTOR, DIRECTOR... AND TEACHER

The skills that make great theater artists can also meet and conquer the challenges you face in the classroom. Theater skills are *human* skills. They help us rekindle play, make up for that lost recess time, and reinforce the collaborative bonds we need—and crave—in life. Most important for us, these skills come in awfully handy in the classroom, for both educators and students. Collaboration, support, and ensemble building defeats fear. Let's look at the concepts that develop and build these skills, why they work, and how we can begin to practice them to create a supportive and collaborative environment in our classroom.

The following skills are the essential core principles for theater makers, and for any teacher (or any person who works in a collaborative field, really). You'll likely recognize some or all of these; perhaps you've simply used different terms, and you may already employ these concepts in your daily work. Even if these ideas are familiar, the analyses and exercises will help you focus and strengthen them even further and enable you to apply them in all of your classes.

## Building Trust in the Classroom

When actors walk into a rehearsal room, they meet their colleagues for the first time. They've only seen the director at the audition. They've never met any of their fellow cast members. The actors have scripts in hand and are called to start Act I, Scene 1, and they have to trust that whatever they offer their partner in the scene will be enough. Through that trust, they make a choice, and then another, and then another. The work begins.

In the classroom, the teacher also needs to establish an environment of trust and show the students that they can trust the teacher. This is not only to educate them but also to establish an environment where it's safe to try things: to raise a hand and answer a question, to actively participate in group work, and to trust themselves while studying for a test and writing a paper.

Sometimes establishing that environment can take time, especially if their fear has grown due to negative past experiences. Perhaps a teacher in the past embarrassed them in front of the room, or they were mocked by fellow students for asking a particular question about a concept they misunderstood.

They need to learn to trust in those relationships as much as trust in themselves. It takes a little time and effort to build trust and get students active and engaged, but once it happens, the classroom atmosphere changes, and the courage and confidence that students build while taking more risks will galvanize everyone, including you. Us vs. Them begins to become the collaborative nature of *we*.

## Yes And Builds a Respectful and Generous Give-and-Take Relationship

One of the most important aspects of theater comes from the improvisational rule of Yes And. In improvisation, Yes And means when one actor offers an idea, the second actor accepts that offer—*and* builds on that offer by adding additional information or ideas. What they contribute or add is the *and*.

For example, if Tom is on stage and points at the sky and yells, "Look out! That duck is flying right toward us!" Mary looks where he's pointing and says, "Oh no! It's getting closer! (*yes*). Is it . . . is it carrying a bomb in its beak?" (*and*). Without the rule of Yes And, Mary might look where Tom's pointing and say, "That's not a duck. I think you need new glasses." This would leave Tom without anywhere to go with the scene—with no additional offer for Mary. The story stops cold.

Yes And encourages students to offer ideas in class discussions, to believe that they and their ideas will be listened to and accepted and are essential to the progression of the discussion. This practice helps them get past nervousness of studying for or taking a test, and to work together on group projects. It helps teachers to better collaborate with students who are reluctant to speak up or participate, or who aren't doing their best work.

## Listening and Being Present

Yes And works when actors are present and listening. When Roger is rehearsing a scene with Rebecca, he needs to be present, in the moment, and listening to her. What did she say, how did she say it, and how does this inform and shape his response? He needs to listen and allow the response to come truthfully. This, of course, connects immediately to listening in class—to the teacher as well as the other students.

It's so easy for an actor to get "stuck in his head" or to think about all the possible nooks and crannies of his performance and his life rather than being present in the moment. Roger may be thinking, "What do I do with my hands while I'm walking toward Rebecca?" To an audience, those actions wouldn't look real or connected to character. They'd look as if Roger is walking across the stage thinking about his hands rather than needing something from Rebecca.

How often are students not listening in the classroom? They might be quiet, eyes on you, pens rapidly jotting notes, and yet you know they're not really taking in any of the information. Or when you ask a question or present a problem, they don't respond. They're thinking, *I need to apologize to my girlfriend after class.* Or, *I hope I make it to work on time.*

In that moment, you might assume (understandably) the whole class didn't do the reading for homework. In actuality, they're not listening because something beyond your control is pulling their focus. If whatever is happening in the classroom isn't pulling them back into the lesson, what can you do—that *is* within your control—to reconnect those students to you, the material, and the room itself?

You begin to nurture listening by *you* listening more, first and foremost, and applying Yes And to class discussions. When students are encouraged to listen—and notice your connection to them—they trust their impulses and act on them, are present and engaged, and like the actor, get out of their heads and into the moment. Instead of thinking, *will this be on the test?* students will have spontaneous questions and comments connected to the lesson at hand.

When a student gives a wrong answer to your question (which can certainly be as discouraging to the student as it is to you and the class discussion), you can redirect the information itself: "Yes, and while George Washington didn't actually chop down a cherry tree, why do you think so many people believe he did? Why is that myth important to American history?" It's more important for the student to believe their contribution matters, even if it might take them a few tries to "get it." Add some of the collaborative techniques included in later chapters, and they'll begin to listen more, be present, and start to trust you, their classmates, and themselves.

## Imagination's Role in Class Lessons and Discussions

To truly get to the heart of theater as play, students need to use their imaginations as much as their teachers. They tend to get locked into a rigid routine of sitting at a desk, listening to a lecture, taking notes, doing an assignment, and taking a quiz, rinse and repeat. But they—and their teachers—have so much more to offer, and that begins with encouraging and nurturing use of imagination.

We do this by first creating an environment that differs from a traditional classroom, or from the type of learning environment students are used to and tired of. Once students realize they're not going to slouch through another lecture, they begin firing on additional imaginative cylinders. We continue to nurture this initial spark by offering assignments that encourage imaginative thinking, and therefore learning.

Instead of learning the dates and times and individuals involved in the signing of the Declaration of Independence, what if they could imagine what it was like to be there? Ask your students what current school policies they disagree with, and have them draft a document publicly disagreeing with them. Have them sign it, but ask how it felt to sign that paper, to go on the record as rebelling against the status quo, knowing the potential consequences?

Instead of showing a movie about the moon landing, the students could put themselves there, to feel low gravity and see the earth from thousands of miles away. Play David Bowie's "Space Oddity," and ask them to respond to it. How do they feel about Major Tom's story, or how Bowie tells it?

These activities will allow students to experience the power and breadth of their imaginations, and they'll learn to connect them to creativity, original thinking, and entrepreneurial skills—creating a generation of innovators through play and theater work.

## HOW COLLABORATIVE SKILLS LEAD TO TEAMWORK

Theater artists collaborate together, sacrificing their shining moment for the *goal's* shining moment: to try out ideas, explore possibilities, and see where the process takes them. Part of this process requires theater artists to eliminate the competitive idea of "my voice is more important. Look at me. I'm the best." The process of creating theater dies if it even momentarily veers into a competitive state. Us vs. Them will kill a play before it leaves the page. Theater, as a collaborative art, allows us to work together to meet an end goal, to tell a story, and to succeed and meet our collective outcomes together.

Collaboration leads to students who want to connect, listen, try out ideas, and *learn*. It can create a far more rewarding result for educators who get to step away from the lecture for a while and start to figure out more effective ways to work together to teach their lessons. True collaboration takes the weight of "problem solver" off the teacher and spreads it throughout the room, giving the students more ownership of, and interest in, the process of learning.

Education becomes rewarding for student *and* teacher because it has become a creative process of discovery and risk taking that leads to true understanding of the material. Students aren't afraid of taking those risks because they now know they won't be mocked and they're more confident that their contribution will be welcomed in the collaboration. You'll grow as well, becoming more observant of the nature of your students' behavior, and how they're engaging in your lessons, all of which will inject new life into your practice. It ensures *passion* is a vital part of teaching and learning, stimulating inspiration and imagination.

## CREATE STRONG, SPECIFIC OBJECTIVES AND COMMIT TO THOSE GOALS

You walk into a classroom with a planned objective for the day; you do this all the time. Often, you'll write it on the board at the beginning of class as a succinct, specific statement: "How to Structure an Essay." Or "The Components of the Lung." Students can see what will be covered for the day before the class even begins.

Conversely, if a director, during rehearsal, dictates the objective to an actor, it can ruin the process for the entire ensemble. Actors need objectives, of course, but that's not the problem. An actor playing a character needs to figure out what that character needs through their own individual exploration and discovery. Superman needs to save Lois. Dorothy needs to find her way home.

The actor determines these objectives by experiencing the role throughout the rehearsal process, creating an investment in and ownership of the character. They figure out—through trial and error, collaborative discussions, trusting impulses, and taking risks—what the objective is, how to commit to it throughout the performance, and how to keep it specific and clearly defined for themselves, their acting partners, and the eventual audience.

So, just as a director can't walk into a room and say, "Larry, Hamlet needs to kill his uncle. That's your objective. Now act," a teacher can't just walk into a room and say, "You need to understand how to outline an essay. Now, take some notes" and expect the students to commit to that objective on their own impulses.

They need to explore the topic and ideas in the classroom, with the teacher and classmates, defuse the fears they may have, and nurture confidence in learning that will allow them to discover (1) what the objective is, (2) how to commit to it, and (3) how to clearly define it, specifically, for themselves. Because you will have created an environment of trust, students will be more comfortable in exploring these ideas through a give-and-take process with one another.

By gaining a more motivated ownership of their education, a stronger understanding of course material, and a healthier response to issues of fear, risk, listening, and engagement, students learn *how* to learn, and that can help them find a career they will enjoy and be called to, which will make them successful in their futures.

## WHAT YOU HAVE

You may already be practicing some of the ideas we've described, or you may have those ideas percolating merrily in your mind but simply haven't yet taken the risk of trying them. You might also be wondering how all this could possibly work. You can begin with the simple—and sometimes elusive—step of focusing on what is already available to you: your powerful imagination, your skills and experience, your desire to create a positive learning environment, and now, a wish to erase any dividing lines that contribute to an Us-vs.-Them relationship.

*Chapter Two*

# The Teacher as Performance Artist

Performers are masters at crossing thresholds, drawing people into their work, and erasing divides between people through the power of storytelling. They begin by connecting with their ideas and emotions, and then creating intersections among self, character, and story. After synthesizing those elements, they draw audiences into that story so they can experience, share, and learn together.

Teachers create a goal for each lesson; we craft our choices for how we're going to tell the story and then personally, verbally, and physically embody that story while engaging our students so they can experience, share, and learn together. Actors benefit from extensive training with multiple approaches to develop skills to effectively create shared experiences. Teachers also strive to create a personal process that is effective, repeatable, and sustainable. A deeper understanding of an actor's methods can offer new ideas to support that process—in abundance. In this chapter, we'll outline how to adapt and apply an actor's process to your own to help you access your innate performance skills needed for your teaching.

## BASICS

Teachers start each semester with a comprehensive self-assessment and a plan of action to build upon. This plan gives a powerful framework and map to follow throughout the course. What does this groundwork look like if you approach it like a performer, whether you're experienced or a beginner?

An actor's training generally includes the development of physical and vocal skills, the ability to research and analyze character and text, personal self-examination, processes to release impulses and imagination, and methods that enable them to commit to and connect with collaborators. Their starting point is usually self-assessment and analysis. Understanding where and who they are in the moment informs what they need to strengthen and develop further.

The great acting teachers, from Konstantin Stanislavski to Viola Spolin, have passed down wildly different theater techniques for generations. No matter which approach an actor chooses, these pathways share a common goal: to give the actor an understanding of the self as storyteller and provide foundational skills to bring truth to characters, power to stories, and connection to acting partners and to the spectator who has come to hear that story. This process begins by encouraging the actor to ask questions of themselves and their character:

- Who am I?
- What character traits does this role require me to create?
- What is the story, and why does it need to be told?
- What is my relationship with others in the play?
- What is my character's goal?
- When is all this happening?
- What do I want? What obstacles are in my way? What are the consequences of not getting what I want?
- How do I physically and vocally prepare for the demands of this role?

You may use some or all these techniques to explore yourself, the teacher, as a performance artist. To help you apply them, we've organized them into three categories: personal analysis, physical preparation, and vocal preparation.

## PERSONAL PERFORMANCE CATEGORY 1: PERSONAL ANALYSIS

### Who Am I as a Teacher?

Whatever drew you to teaching is indelibly connected to who you are as a human being. It can be a challenge to focus on our personal traits, so if you find yourself struggling, try this: If you were asked to describe yourself to someone who was about to meet "you" for the first time, which qualities should they know about you? Write them down. Now, look back at that list. Which personal traits feel most connected to your passion for teaching? Can you draw a line between certain qualities and your journey to becoming a teacher? Examples:

- I'm curious by nature and always loved school and learning.

- I'm a nurturer at heart; I love nothing more than seeing lightbulbs go off for young people and knowing that I helped guide them to those discoveries.
- I'm a caretaker and have always found myself "acting the parent." I enjoy teaching others about responsibility and have good instincts on how to hold young people accountable to take responsibility themselves.
- A teacher changed my life for the better; I want to give that back in every way possible.

## Which of My Personal Traits Are Needed in My Role as a Teacher?

When was the last time you gave yourself the time and space to reflect on your unique strengths? This is a little different from the personal traits listed above (though they may be connected). What special skills do you carry with you, no matter where, what, or when you teach or how many students are before you? What makes you *you* as a teacher? Examples:

- I'm very physical, and I've been told that if my hands were tied behind my back, I wouldn't be able to talk! I get excited when I teach and gesture a lot. I know my students imitate me when I'm not around, but it always seems to be with good humor.
- I'm a strong storyteller; I know how to lay out the steps of a story that lead to the climax, and I know how to add details to keep a listener engaged.
- I'm very adaptable; if a lesson isn't going as planned, I'm able to quickly shift gears and make it appear as if that was my intention all along.
- I'm a quick thinker. If something goes awry in class, I'm able to respond in a way that addresses the potential problem that lies ahead.

## What Is the Story of This Class?

Teachers are storytellers, whether they're bringing to life the principles of tectonic plates or describing the mysteries of ancient cultures. What story will be told in this course? What is the crucial information you must impart? How does that story grow from class to class? If we think of the story, and how we want to tell it week by week, we may find a far more interesting approach, drawing in those listeners gathered around the fire. Think about "the old days" of watching or reading a story that was broken down to a weekly serial. What made you hungry for the next installment? The cliffhanger. Some examples of storytelling cliffhanger questions you can pose to students to keep them connected to course material:

- This story is about the geological forces that created the continents as we know them (tectonic plates, planet Earth). What happened to our own geographic area when North America first ripped itself from Laurasia?
- This class is the story of the conflicts that led to the American Civil War. What was the key moment just before the first shell was fired over Fort Sumter?
- This is our origin story: the birth of our universe and how we came to be. How do we understand the Big Bang event? How do we feel about Neil deGrasse Tyson's description: "We are atomically connected to all atoms in the universe. We are not figuratively, but literally stardust" (2008)?

## Why Does This Story Need to Be Told?

Not "it's a requirement for the major," but why is this story/class needed by the students, and by you? By conveying information as story, you give your students a greater investment in the material. Instead of "students should write this down because it's going to be on the test," why is this story vital in their present lives? For example:

- So students can understand the role their daily actions play in climate change
- So they can learn to express their ideas and thoughts more clearly

What would happen if the story *didn't* get told? In theater terms, what's at stake? What would be lost? For example, the musical *Hair* was produced at the height of the Vietnam War; it focuses on one individual's journey from being drafted to being killed. We're swept up in Claude's journey from the moment he gets his draft notice, and follow his turmoil as to whether he should go, or run away to Canada and never see his tribe—his family— again. In the end, he leaves for war, and he's killed. We experience his loss and witness his community's response to that loss as they sing "Let the Sunshine In," a plea for enlightenment and change, so that another human life isn't taken in a war.

Songs from *Hair* became anthems for antiwar protests, and the music and story contributed to—and some would say, fueled—the national dialogue about whether to withdraw American troops or continue to fight the war in Vietnam. Though it still resonates today, *Hair* was a story that needed to be told at that precise moment in time.

As you examine your course, what is happening in your community, state, country, and world around you and your students right now? How does the content specifically resonate? Why is this class needed at this precise moment in time?

What's in the cultural zeitgeist at this moment to help you connect the story to your students? You may find a cultural archetype your students will forever connect with. You can adjust the story to fit the needs of an ever-changing world.

## What Is My Relationship to This Story, and to the Students?

We don't always get to teach the material we feel most connected to. How do you feel about the material you've been asked to teach? Does it excite you? The subject matter may be like an old friend: a warm, welcoming presence you feel at home with. Or the content may be like an old adversary: you know it well, but you just don't like it. If the subject isn't your area of specialty, how can you find a way in? How can you transform your feelings into a learning opportunity for you and a more interesting approach to connect with your students? Examples:

- I love the Neolithic time period and am excited to teach about the British Isles during this era. I'm confident I can instill my enthusiasm in my students because of the mystery that surrounds many of the stone monuments and structures the cultures left behind.

    - Solution: Keep doing what you're doing!

- I have a fraught relationship with Freshman Writing Seminar. I appreciate the need for the course, and how essential it is for our students, but it bores me to tears. I've taught it many times and need to find a fresh way in so that my boredom isn't contagious.

    - Solution: I'll have them select a range of topics to choose from popular culture; then I'll be surprised by the topic, and they'll be engaged by writing about a favorite singer, filmmaker or YouTube personality.

- I can talk for hours about advanced algebraic equations, but my students dread it. I'll find a way to connect it to them and ensure that my own enthusiasm is contagious.

    - Solution: In preparing this class, I'll prepare myself physically and mentally by using some of the techniques discussed later in this chapter.

- I can read Shakespeare's text and understand the key points at a glance, but my students will need some extra help that goes beyond just defining terms. How can I give them ownership over the text so they explore it on their own and find joy in the discoveries?

- Solution: I'll ask them to read *Troilus and Cressida*, and their assignment will be to identify as many insults as possible from the text, define their meaning, and design a game to reveal which team of readers has gleaned the most insults.

## What Is My Personal Goal?

You became a teacher for a reason. What do you want from teaching this particular class? Start the sentence with "I want . . ." (See chapter 5 on how to focus and create objectives via the actor's process.) Continue to work on and develop your objective, and focus on active verbs that resonate for you. If you find yourself leaning toward the negative ("the students will *never* do that"), focus on active verbs to make the objective a reality. Examples:

- I want the students to engage in the joy of Shakespeare's plays.
- I want to enhance the students' ability to express themselves clearly in their writing.
- I want the students to present an inspiring speech without reading it from a sheet of paper.

## What Time Is the Course Scheduled? How Might That Impact My Effectiveness and the Student's Ability to Learn?

Every person has their own unique biological clock. Teaching an 8:00 a.m. course is different from one that starts at 10:00 a.m., which is different yet again from a 7:00 p.m. class. What time of day do you feel your sharpest? What adjustments could you make to be at your best for this particular class?

The stereotype of students dreading an early Monday morning class is pretty accurate; same for an evening class, which is often populated by mature students with work and family obligations. How does the hour of the day affect their learning? You can be creative with adjustments to combat—and compensate—for the challenges that the scheduled time presents.

In my undergraduate college, I enrolled in an evening American history course, 6:00 p.m. to 9:30 p.m. meeting time. There were about ten of us in the group, and we were all coming either from a full day of other classes or, for the continuing ed students, from a full day at work. At the first class, we were all pretty listless, hands on chins and slumped in chairs. Our professor was a dynamic instructor who had a passion for the material and a deep respect for those of us who had registered for his evening course. He was wonderful—but it wasn't enough to rally us.

He stopped his lecture at one point and said point blank: "I understand this is a difficult time of day; you're tired, I get it, but we can't change the meeting time. What could make this better for you?" One person cheekily said, "A pot of coffee would be nice." The professor said, "Terrific! I'll bring the coffee pot from our lounge next week. Would someone volunteer to pick up milk and sugar, and we can all kick in for the cost?" Someone volunteered. As a joke, I said, "I can bring my popcorn maker so we can have snacks." He smiled and said, "I love popcorn. A healthy treat, please bring that next week." And so on.

At the next class, we had fresh coffee and popcorn, and as the semester went on, people also brought other "comforts of home" (cookies, tea and honey, etc.). It changed everything. His willingness to acknowledge the obstacle and collaborate with us on finding solutions deepened our investment in the course and the material—and it helped us with the very real physical and mental challenges of having a long class at the end of the day. We became engaged and lively, the atmosphere felt less "formal," and it felt more as if we were having great conversations with friends at that late hour.

## What Surrounds Me?

The environment we teach in has a significant impact on our state of mind. No matter what space we enter, we get a specific feeling from it. Imagine a room with high ceilings, brightly colored walls, and large windows, with a balanced "Goldilocks" temperature (not too cold or hot). Now imagine a room with low ceilings made of old acoustic tiles from the 1970s, industrial green walls, and stuffy air. It's crazy to deny we'd prefer to teach in the first room. If we become more observant about our environment, and intentional about working with those given circumstances, we can have more control over our success in the class.

Note your first response when you get your room assignment for the semester. Are you delighted? What is it about that space that gives you a good feeling? By contrast, do you feel cheated? Is it a claustrophobic basement classroom? Familiarize yourself with as many details of the room as possible. How can you use those details to your advantage? If your list feels negative to you, what can you change?

- Start by simply accepting the reality of the space. Find moments to acknowledge those shortcomings of the environment with the students (as the professor acknowledged the shortcomings about time in the earlier story).
- If the room feels confining, take five-minute breaks each hour to stretch; take a short walk in the hallway and return a bit refreshed. Side note: Make sure the students leave their cell phones behind. If the purpose is to break free of a confined space, there's nothing more confining than needing to check the latest text or tweet.
- If the color of the walls is institutional green, can you use humor in the material you're teaching? "The assignment this week was to read about the Battle of Bataan in World War II; they've thoughtfully assigned us to General MacArthur's original classroom for inspiration."
- Most important, ask the students, "What *could* make this better?"

If you're all feeling a little oppressed by the physical space, exercise your imaginations together to get a feeling of control over the circumstances. You can make something that *seemed* beyond your control—better.

## What Do You Want/Need from the Students?

Actors are successful when they intentionally work from "the positive" instead of the negative—that is, playing what they *do* want, instead of playing what they *don't* want. Have you ever found yourself thinking, *I hope they don't fall asleep today* or *I don't want them to hate organic chemistry*. Flip those thoughts, and play the positive: what *do* you want?

Actors also know that they can't project a condition onto their partner. That is, it's not fair to say, "I want the students to be happy and interested." That may be true, but that's a desire instead of a goal, and not "playable." You *can*, however, commit to an *objective* that may *result* in happiness and interest. The question is, what do you want *from* them?

The objective should engage you with your partner. "I want her to apologize," "I want him to admit he lied," and so on. Actors become stronger by making their objectives active and by fighting hard to get what they want. "I want" is a dynamic (and enjoyable) objective that you can play in the classroom. It challenges you to home in on a specific objective; you may start with something that's true but isn't that interesting or active.

And if *you're* feeling bored with the objective, imagine how the students feel. Examples of passive objectives:

- I want them to *understand*.
- I just want *to tell* them about this subject.

These statements may be *true*, but they're not *active*. Also, note anytime you find yourself uttering the word "just"—it's an apology word that negates the intention you associate with it. That is, "just" feels as if you've already received pushback about the thing you want, and you're minimizing why you wanted it in the first place. Examples of active objectives:

- I want them to engage in the class discussion.
- I want them to demonstrate they're grasping the material.
- I want them to volunteer to come to the front of the room.

## What Potential Blocks Are in My Way? What Can I Do to Address Them?

These blocks could be personal to you, with students, or with your administration. How do you respond to obstacles? Are you a glass-half-empty or a glass-half-full person? (Or as a friend once said, "What glass?") We can get discouraged when confronting multiple blocks. The good news is, there's always something you can do about it. If your reaction to that sentence was "Ha! You've never taught at *my* school," then you're probably a "glass-half-empty" person.

Try to look for more reasons to *do* something than reasons *not* to do something. Empower yourself by knowing that even small things—while they may not remove the obstacle entirely—can make a significant difference and free up your ability to teach in that moment.

Potential blocks and solutions:

- The class size is much larger than what I'm used to; I'll need to adjust my physical and vocal approach to ensure that I'm able to connect with this large number of students.
- The subject matter is pretty dense; I'll need to find creative ways to make the material accessible for the students to grasp it.
- I'm a last-minute replacement for this class, and the subject isn't my specialty. I won't have time to prepare, or to confer with the previous instructor. I will plan the first class, then call a colleague(s) who specializes in the material, meet with them, and accept that I'll need to "catch up" in between the following classes.

Potential blocks with students and ways to tackle them (the blocks, not the students!):

- This is a required course for a major, and it has a reputation for being difficult. Students have increased anxiety about grades and assignments.

  - I'll acknowledge on the first day that "the reputation" exists and will have an open and honest discussion about the challenges of the course. I'll give students reassurances about what I'll do to help them meet those challenges and express my faith in their ability to succeed.

- The students spend an inordinate amount of time on their smartphones, which steals their focus and concentration in class.

  - I'll create a digital device policy for our time together and a method to determine everyone's participation.

- I'm younger than many of the graduate students enrolled; I worry they won't respect me.

  - I'll reflect on the source of my fear and anxiety. I'll consider why I was assigned this course and the confidence my department chair has in my expertise. I'll think of ways to respect my abilities more so I won't "feed the beast" of my fear.

**What Actions Can I Take to Get What I Want?**

*Part 1: Actions*

In theater, it's often said that what someone is willing to do to get what they want determines character. After doing the above analysis, you'll have a clearer idea of what makes you *you* and what actions you're willing to take to get what you want from your students. To begin, add *Actions: The Actors' Thesaurus* by Marina Calderone and Maggie Lloyd-Williams to your collection. The authors recommend you assign a specific action to each line of text to help achieve your objective. By determining an action for each moment, actors create a dynamic road map that connects them to the text and to their partners. For example:

- If Theresa is playing a customer in a coffee shop and has to say the line "I'd like a cup of coffee, please" to Joe the Barista, she might add the

action *to rush*, so that she's communicated the need for Joe to hurry in preparing the coffee.
- Or perhaps Joe has typically been slow and she's trying a new action—*to inspire*. It's the same exact line, but the actor is trying a different approach.
- These actions will govern *how* she says the line (and identifies her need through physicality, inflection, listening, and intention) and what it's specifically communicating to her partner in the scene.

Ascribe specific actions to each step in your lesson plan. These will activate you and give you something to *do* and will help you be more present with your students. Open *Actions* to any page, *to convert, to galvanize, to embolden*; these are just a few you find when randomly searching. For each new idea/point in your lesson plan, assign an action to it. Actors describe a unit of action as a "beat"—a beat isn't very long and lasts until something changes. This could be a change of subject or a new thought, a shift in an interpersonal dynamic, or a new character entering.

You'll need to decide what the beats are in your lesson plan before assigning an action to each one. You can also repeat an action, especially if it helps you achieve your objective and builds the arc of your lesson plan. This is particularly useful during the lecture portions of a class. We're often told not to lecture for an entire class, but for the twenty minutes or so that we need to communicate the material. What actions can we play in that allotted time? We can look to embolden students about their knowledge, to galvanize them for the upcoming quiz, or to excite them about the upcoming group project.

*To give them information* or *to make them understand* are nonspecific, passive actions. Keep your psychological actions precise, and your lecture, group assignment, or class discussion will be more focused and purposeful. What are you willing to do in class to get what you want? Are you willing to bolster, to incite, or to lure?

*Part 2: As If*

If you find yourself struggling with an action, you may be subconsciously rebelling against it, or you may not find the material particularly enthralling. Here's where another acting tool comes in handy: As If. This is when an actor substitutes something they personally care about for something the text requires of them that they may not relate to. They're not changing the text; they're changing what they're feeling while communicating their action.

For example, today your lesson focuses on parliamentary procedure. You *hate* parliamentary procedure; you think it's duller than dirt. What could you substitute to help you engage with the content and with your students? Maybe you love legislative branch powers; so, use the powers of your imagination. While explaining *Robert's Rules of Order*, can it be As If you're actually talking about your passion for legislation? If this sounds like "fake it 'til you make it," you're not wrong, and if it helps the material come alive for you and your students, there's nothing wrong with that either!

*Part 3: Status*

If, even after giving it the proverbial old college try, you still find playing actions difficult, there's another acting concept you can use to get what you want: status.

"Status" can be a tremendous tool in the classroom. We don't mean social or economic class; Keith Johnstone, a former educator and author of the terrific book *Impro*, describes status as an exchange of power in an interaction or relationship, thus creating a hierarchy in that relationship. Dominance and submission are on opposite sides of this seesaw of power exchange, and the active raising or lowering of status creates a pecking order within a hierarchy, with one always higher and one lower.

Status is a part of every human interaction, whether through body language, how we relate to the space around us, or in our vocal and psychological choices. Having the awareness and ability to *intentionally* lower or raise our status to get what we want is a great skill. Johnstone describes someone of high status as "Don't come near me—I bite" and someone playing low status as "Don't bite me; I'm not worth the trouble."

You can have high or low status to another person, to an object, to environment, to time, and even to your own body. Status is the very definition of division; someone has a little more or a little less power than the other person. But *awareness* of the hierarchical power structure—and the choices you make in addressing it—can reduce or eliminate divisions. Now, imagine how applying a specific status to your action can support your goals. For example:

> *Objective*: I want the students to volunteer to come to the front of the classroom.
> 
> *Actions* (throughout specific moments of the lesson plan): *To coax, to embolden, to galvanize, to rally, to tease*. Each of these actions has different flavors, and you know best what actions are more fun for you to play, and what works best with a particular group. Examples:

- You notice that your Advanced Math class is very shy. If you choose *to rally* and play slightly lower status to the students, you look as if you're

having trouble remembering an equation and need them to rally to help *you*. You may succeed in rallying them if they think you're not confident enough to rally yourself.
- If your Intro to Speech students are insecure about public speaking, as so many are, you choose *to embolden*. Play a slightly higher status than the students to illustrate the level of confidence you have in their ability to come to the front of the classroom. "If I can do this every day, you can try it once today." And when they give a speech and you present yourself as an "expert" in assessing their abilities, your confidence could embolden them—even if they're struggling to accept that they were successful in front of the room. If a high-status person has confidence in their ability to get in front of the class, they'll feel safer in doing it.

## What Are the Consequences If I Don't Get What I Want?

This helps you identify the core of what's at stake. Actors are often instructed to "raise the stakes," meaning increase the urgency and importance of their objective. Now, not every class is life or death, but you can identify high stakes in every lesson. Allow that to drive and support your objective, and to inform the actions you take in order to get what you want.

- If my history students don't understand United States Reconstruction, they won't be able to do the assignment I have planned for the civil rights movement.
- My political science students have said they don't intend to vote in the upcoming election, which has state- and local-level, not national, races on the ballot. I need them to grasp the relationship between local and national governments so they can identify how every level of government affects their lives; this could motivate them to vote in every election.
- Last semester, half of my students failed the midterm and I had a miserable experience grading. If I apply more engaging techniques to help them master the material, they'll pass the test, and I'll have a better weekend.
  - This may seem like a consequence of self-interest; however, teachers sometimes contribute to their own overworked conditions. If you're more effective in the classroom, your students' work will be stronger, and you won't spend every waking moment on extensive remarks needing to be made in the grading process.

By doing "Personal Analysis" for each of your courses, you'll create a solid framework that will help you set goals and achieve an honest self-assessment to support you during the semester. It will also help you chart your growth now and throughout your career.

## PERSONAL PERFORMANCE CATEGORY 2: PHYSICAL PREPARATION AND PHYSICAL STORYTELLING FOR THE TEACHER

In addition to the questions that encourage internal exploration, actors also make exciting discoveries by activating their physicality as storytellers. For teachers, the personal questions above may fall neatly into our comfort zone of intellectual weightlifting, but it's only the first step of our three-pronged preparation for performance. Our minds need to bring our bodies along for the ride and enhance our psychological discoveries through physical expression.

Human history tells us that physical storytelling has been a part of our lives for tens of thousands of years. There are beautiful cave paintings in France that depict human figures wearing animal skins, striking curious poses. Images of humans depicting dance and gesture are found on pottery and in the artwork of several ancient civilizations. Physical theater inspires a visceral response in an audience that can be more compelling than oral tradition. Even now, when a common language fails us, we make ourselves understood through gestures or movement.

Physical storytelling has the capacity to move people on a primal level—more universal than language. Because it dynamically stimulates the visual senses, it can spark the viewer's desire to engage more deeply with the story. This makes physical storytelling and gesture one of the most important and powerful weapons in an actor's, and teacher's, arsenal.

We often hear young actors say, "I don't know what to do with my body!" Let's face it, there's a reason millions of books about our relationships to our body and body image have been sold. When an actor is struggling physically, it usually comes down to one of two things: (1) they haven't taken care of their body, or (2) they're unclear about the story they're trying to tell, and they haven't committed to a choice to determine the direction and strength of the story.

How confident are you physically? Teachers are marathon runners *and* sprinters; you're skilled at long-range planning and successfully surviving an academic year. Also, you're sprinters in that when the bell rings at 9:25 a.m., class must begin with energy, focus, and full commitment. Slowly easing into a class that lasts only an hour isn't an option. Well, it *is*—but you'd lose the students' attention pretty quickly.

You need to take care of your body as much as any athlete. Resist defending any unhealthy choices you might be making. ("I'm exhausted after work; I don't have the energy to exercise.") You can't do your job without a relatively healthy body, voice, and psyche. Consider:

- Do you exercise regularly? The American Heart Association recommends 150 minutes per week of moderate-intensity aerobic activity and at least two days per week for muscle-strengthening activities (weights or resistance training).
- How much time do you spend sitting and how much being active? Many organizations recommend ten thousand steps a day, but you can also benefit from seven to eight thousand daily steps.
- How's your nutrition? Do you prepare your own meals or rely on the nearest takeout? Not that prepackaged foods from the local deli can't be healthy, but . . .
- Do you average seven to nine hours of sleep each night? How easily do you fall asleep, and are you able to stay asleep once you do? Most current recommendations are for seven to nine hours a night, but no less than six. We understand that some people are gifted with the ability to sleep for only a few hours a night and can bounce out of bed in the morning refreshed, sharp, and ready to go. We envy you and ask you to keep these recommendations in the back of your mind if you notice changes in your stamina, focus, or immune system over time.
- Do you meditate and/or do deep breathing exercises?

Teaching can be an incredibly stressful job. The recommendations here and in the section on voice may seem like more in a series of onerous tasks that you simply don't have the time for. Try not to let self-care be the thing that you cut from your to-do list. If you don't commit to supporting your well-being, you run the risk of becoming a statistic of teacher burnout.

You barely have time to make coffee and get to work in the morning, so how can you do all this? You *make* the time to be a better teacher, using moments you already have. You can meditate during office hours if no one shows up, walk to your colleague's office instead of emailing or texting them, or take the stairs instead of elevator. If you have a meeting with a colleague, why not take a walk outside while you discuss the issue?

Start with just a few minutes a day, and you'll feel the difference. Regular exercise strengthens your body, helps you stay attuned to your physical self, improves mood, and reduces stress. The Mayo Clinic has an excellent website for those already proficient with exercising and for those who are just starting. Good nutrition supports physical strength and well-being, can reduce risks for heart disease and other conditions, and improves your overall energy.

Sleep is perhaps the unsung hero of this health triad—and is the one many of us forgo if we're behind on papers, or are consumed with mentally replaying some crummy encounter from a faculty meeting. Ironically, we sometimes stay up till the wee hours because late nights are when everyone else has gone to bed and that may be the only time we have to reflect on our self-care. Poor sleep has been connected to a range of conditions from high blood pressure to obesity. Consult with your doctor (not just online sources!) to create a healthy plan of balanced diet and exercise that works for you, and if sleep is your greatest challenge, we recommend the following:

- Stop all online activities (writing, checking email) at least two hours before you go to bed. Current research reveals the screens of devices suppress the production of melatonin, the hormone that drives our sleep cycles (Figueiro et al. 2011). As long as you use your device for work, your brain will associate the need to be alert *for* work when you use it—even if you're checking for personal messages before bedtime.
- Keep all electronic devices out of the bedroom. Don't train your body that the bedroom is also a workroom; train it to know that the bedroom is where you relax and sleep.
- Buy an alarm clock, and use that rather than your smartphone's alarm. The smartphone presents a temptation to respond to messages immediately upon waking; if you wake up in the night, the very presence of a smartphone—or any screens—can stimulate your brain to want to check for messages. Smartphones are designed to trigger the dopamine release (Doucleff and Aubrey 2018)—and unless you're Batman, few reasons exist to answer a signal in the middle of the night. Keep the smartphone in another room, far from your bed. The books and lectures of Dr. Sherry Turkle of MIT give in-depth information on the human relationship to technology, as does *Turn That Thing Off! Collaboration and Technology in 21st-Century Actor Training* by Rose Burnett Bonczek, Roger Manix, and David Storck. Though theater-centric, *Turn That Thing Off!* focuses on the patterns of smartphone/tech use by college students and includes startling revelations about the impact of excessive smartphone use on collaborative and social behaviors and cognitive skills (empathy, listening, awareness, memory, and more).
- If you can't fall asleep, focus on deep breathing, and fully exhale after each inhalation.

Going back to the young actor who didn't know what to do with their body, if you're taking care of your body and mind with a healthy balance of exercise, good nutrition, and adequate sleep, your physical choices will be grounded, supportive, and integrated with any task.

## PERSONAL PERFORMANCE CATEGORY 3: VOCAL PREPARATION

It's happened to every teacher. Class is minutes away from starting. You're in your office, having just finished grading assignments and entering the grades into your book. You're looking over the agenda for the day and ask the eternal question: "Wait, what am I about to teach?" You see that it's a day that involves lots of you (lecture, guided assignments) and less of them (no group or individual work, no quizzes or reading from textbooks). It's all about you.

And you're exhausted. Your voice is pushed to its limit after weeks of teaching, trying to shake off that winter cold, or yelling at the television during the news hour. You ask yourself, "How am I going to do this?"

Vocal warm-ups are one of the most important aspects of actor training. They help the actor access every part of their instrument, from the lowest bass to the highest tenor, to be able to say every line with the precision and clarity required of them in each rehearsal and performance. Yet for some reason, many teachers don't give this a moment's thought. We shrug, walk into the classroom with our coffee or tea, and our voice cracks on a simple attempt at "good morning."

Vocal preparation is vital for teachers who are about to command a room full of learners who may not be ready to fulfill their side of the bargain. We need to walk in the room able to use the power of our voice, to ensure that "good morning" is a transformative introductory moment enthusiastically shaping the trajectory of the entire lesson. Voice work can also be intensely personal. Your voice is part of your identity, an audible signature of who you are. Try not to judge your current vocal skills. Nothing about your voice is "bad"; you may simply have some assets you haven't fully developed to your best advantage.

You may want to take voice work further—and if so, kudos! Just as there are loads of books about actor training, there are as many about voice training. Cicely Berry, Kristin Linklater, and Patsy Rodenburg have excellent books about voice and speech. You can also find videos online demonstrating exercises to develop your voice. We've outlined a series of simple exercises in appendix P to get you started and encourage you to include them in your practice.

Again, we understand how little time you have for anything "extra," but some of the exercises in the appendices are ones you could easily do in your car, or as you're walking to the subway (well, maybe not sticking your tongue out). You can do *some* for even a few minutes a day. Vocal training is the same as body training; if you do only ten minutes of aerobics each week, you won't feel or look like the people in the commercials. If you can do five to fifteen minutes at least a few times a week, you'll notice a difference in your strength and vocal stamina.

## BRINGING IT ALL TOGETHER

The first time you try to integrate these new processes into your work, you might feel you're trying to pat your head and rub your tummy at the same time. A combination of preparation, time, patience, and practice is the actor's *and* the teacher's tried and true method to synthesize anything new. The following is an example of how one teacher might bring all of those elements together.

## SAMPLE LESSON PLAN WITH APPLICATION OF ALL THREE CATEGORIES

Lesson Plan: "Text Message People in a Cover Letter World" (based on Christian De Matteo's Writing Lab exercise)

### Category 1: Personal Analysis

1. *Why am I a teacher?* I grew up in challenging circumstances, and having strong teachers empowered me and changed my life. I'm compelled to empower and teach students to give back what was given to me.
2. *What makes you the unique teacher that you are?* I love knowledge, I'm a good storyteller, and I'm irreverent and have a good sense of humor and a quick wit. I'm able to make serious points while getting my students to laugh.
3. *What is the story of this class?* How to become strong, expressive writers and communicate effectively in that medium.
4. *Why does this story need to be told?* Current technology and social media used by this generation of students has created different modes of written expression (texts, emojis, etc.). Writing, structure, and grammar as skill sets have become weaker; what's taught in the classroom is not how students are being trained to communicate in writing by their devices. Students are losing the ability to express themselves fully in writing and to be aware of nuances in tone and meaning.
5. *What is my relationship to this story and to the students?* I want my students to express themselves and their ideas fully now and in their futures. I want them to communicate who they are and what they think in a professional and comprehensive way, and the ability to write effectively will likely be essential to their future work.

6. *What is your personal goal?* I want my students to have a successful future and career.
7. *What time is it?* 6:00 p.m. Many of my students work at day jobs and arrive after a full shift at their places of employment. Presently, college students primarily communicate by texts, so this moment of time in our society is an important factor in this lesson.
8. *What surrounds me?* I'm in a writing lab room with chalkboard and whiteboard. The class is relatively modern, with good light and decent air quality.
9. *What do you want from your students?* To express who they are and what they need in clear, precise, engaging terms. Then, to apply these concepts to their English class essays and research papers, as well as their career development course's cover letters, résumés, and other business communication, so they can build up to real-world written communication, earning them jobs in which they will excel.
10. *What potential blocks are in my way?* Students may feel the ability to express one's self in writing is "old school," something they won't really need for their futures (doesn't everybody text?). They may also feel the lesson implies a rejection of their cultures and activities online.

*What Will I Do to Meet These Obstacles?*

I'll discuss cover letters and the important role they play in getting a job. This will illustrate that I have their best interests, and their future, at heart. I'll point out their letters need to be grammatically perfect while clearly and concisely telling the potential employer who they are, why they want to work for them, and why they should want to work with the student.

Additionally, they need to be interesting, even clever or insightful, to stand out from the stack that the human resources manager or employer will eventually need to traverse to whittle the pile down to three to five interviews. If their cover letter contains errors or makes them sound boring, and yet reflects "their best work," then they won't be considered. Strengthening their writing skills then becomes an essential, and very learnable, skill to develop for the sake of their futures.

*What Actions Will I Take to Get What I Want?*

I'll ask them to share text language they know (*to reassure, to bolster, to stimulate*). I know a lot of the lingo and will prepare some anecdotes (*to encourage, to inspire, to inflame*). I'll ask, what acronyms do you use when you text your friends? When you post on social media? (*to enliven, to validate, to permit*). I'll have them write their answers on the board: TTYL, BRB, SMH (*to acknowledge, to accept, to befriend*).

Eventually we'll get to ILY. I love you. We'll discuss the nature of love, and I'll lead them to the conclusion that love must be one of the most profound expressions you could give to another, and we're diminishing it down to three letters: ILY (*to unearth, to reveal*).

To reinforce this, I will assign them into groups of two. I'll ask them to make eye contact and say the acronym to one another. Then, holding that eye contact, they'll say the actual two to four words and then expand those two to four words to become a complete sentence that fully communicates the meaningful phrase. We'll then debrief as a class and discuss the changes in their experiences and emotions between the acronym and the complete statement.

For older students I may use similar exercises for WTF (what the fuck). We'll discuss how many uses there are in the English language for that word—nouns, verbs, and adjectives—and how the acronym diminishes each one of those uses (*to guide, to unearth*).

I'll plan my conclusion to the discussion, and I'll start with questions to lead them to it, so I won't lecture. "How does writing in acronyms affect the need to express yourself fully?" (*to embolden, to coax, to stir*). In these discussions, students will draw the conclusion that text messaging language encourages a limitation on expression for the purpose of speed and convenience over substance.

I'll conclude with making the following point: writing, whether a cover letter, an English paper, a report, or a story, needs to be concise but profound. It should be grammatically correct but also feel like a person, not a robot, is communicating something human. I'll challenge the students to go from being text-message people to cover-letter writers, able to express who they are and what they need in clear, precise, interesting, and human terms (*to empower, to embolden, to inspire*).

## Category 2: Physical Preparation and Physical Storytelling for the Teacher

This is going to be a dynamic class; there's the potential for students to use their phones for something other than the lesson, so I want to move throughout the lesson and be in close physical proximity to supervise their actions. I'll balance this goal when I encourage the students to write their own examples. Additionally, the class meets at 6:00 p.m., and I'll have a long break between my 1:00 class and this one. This will make for a long and physically demanding day.

I'll go to bed earlier the night before and ensure seven to eight hours of sleep. I'll make a healthy lunch to bring, along with a piece of fruit for a snack, so I can be fueled for the 6:00 class. I'll take a brisk walk outside between classes so I can absorb some vitamin D and connect with nature.

Additionally, I'll carve out ten minutes prior to the class for some light stretches in my office.

## Category 3: Vocal Preparation

This class is going to involve some lecture and a good deal of discussion, and the late hour of the class means I will have been using my voice for many hours before I even get to the class. In between classes, I'll give myself some vocal rest; if I take a walk outside for thirty to forty minutes in between classes, I can achieve both vocal rest and physical exercise. In addition to devoting ten minutes to some light stretches before class, I'll add five to seven minutes of some vocal exercises. Some tongue stretches, breath work, and light humming to open up my resonators (throat, mouth, and nasal cavities to strengthen my vocal resonance and flexibility) can be enough.

I need to guarantee that I'll have the vocal muscularity and power to lead this three-hour evening class. Also, given the subject matter, there may be excitement and a bit of chaos in students talking over one another. Having the full range of my voice will prevent any temptation of yelling (hopefully!) or vocal strain to redirect the students and their enthusiasm.

## THE STRONG PERFORMANCE

It doesn't take long to follow these three steps for each class. The more you do them, the more they'll become an integral part of your foundation. You'll have greater self-awareness, clearer and more creative ideas on how to teach, and the physical and vocal strength to activate your choices. The more intentional you are with your choices, the stronger your performance will be in the classroom. And that's the point: you'll be able to analyze, create, and activate your work as dynamic performance, regardless of what subject you teach—or which story you're telling.

This is not to suggest you're lacking in any of these skills, or haven't been trying variations already. You were already a performer, long before you read this chapter. These concepts offer you options when you think, *I don't know why, but I was really off*, or *That could have gone better*. What we're describing can give you a repeatable and sustainable system to be consistently successful in practice. The next step is to apply those time-tested teaching skills to the most important activity of every good performer: telling a good story.

*Chapter Three*

# Creating the Story

In 2018, Marvel Studios released the first of their two-part epic story, *Avengers: Infinity War*. Audiences flocked to see it, selling out theaters and breaking box office records. Those who hadn't seen the movie yet were left wondering, *What could be so shocking?* We know this story. Heroes gather to face an adversary. They almost lose. At the last minute, they win, save the day, celebrate, and live to fight another day. (Spoiler warning!)

Except it didn't happen like that.

Moviegoers were instead greeted with an epic adventure in which our heroes did, indeed, gather to face an adversary, but in the end, that adversary, the Titan Thanos, gathered the Infinity Stones, snapped his gauntleted fingers, and wiped out half of all living things. Thanos sat on a sunny hillside looking over his new home, smiling in the face of victory. At the end of the credits, moviegoers were given one final gut punch: "Thanos will return" in big block letters.

We were all surprised. Hurt. Betrayed. We loved it. It turned out that this movie delivered on its promise, but our expectations were offset. What we didn't know was that the "hero" of the movie wasn't the Avengers. It was Thanos the whole time. But what does Thanos have to do with teaching in a classroom full of students? Is it that we all wish, from time to time, we could snap our fingers, turn half of them to dust, and continue our lesson to the rest of them, who either love what we're doing or are so grateful not to be dusted that they'll do anything we say?

Well, maybe.

The journey of Thanos in *Avengers* was a *good story*. It had interesting motivations, a strong start, fun and challenging obstacles and complications along the way, and an epic conclusion. More importantly, it took a step beyond audience expectations. It didn't subvert them but instead gave us a better story than we expected, and one unlike any other story being told at that time. Audiences expected an adventure where the good guys fought the bad guys and won. The filmmakers gave us something *even better*.

Our students expect us to be a teacher, a lecturer, a grader, someone who will judge them based on everything they do, and someone who holds their GPA in their fingers for the entire semester and who has the power to turn them into dust. Many of them expect us to show up, write some notes on the board, talk about those notes for a few minutes, give them a handout and some time to do it, and follow it up with a homework assignment.

What if we showed up and, instead of presenting a lecture or a handout, brought our students a *lesson-as-story*? What if instead of Avengers, we brought Thanos? We'd bring a really good story with all the outcomes and assignments we already planned but elevated in a presentation they'd have to acknowledge, from the beginning, wasn't the story they expected—it was even better.

A change in the delivery of our lesson, in the storytelling structure, would be enough to breach the dividing line between the content we need to deliver and the imagination of our students—and our ability to jump-start that imagination. Become an engaged and engaging storyteller, newly in touch with your performance skills, and craft a story specifically for these listeners in a strong and dynamic way.

This chapter will discuss the concepts of story and connect them to teaching, and include suggestions for applying storytelling techniques to classroom strategies. We'll answer the big, important question: How do you get students invested in the lesson in the same way they invest in their favorite stories? How do you get them to care about the soldiers in the War of 1812? How do you get them personally involved in the outcome of Kafka's "In the Penal Colony"? And how do you ensure they surprise themselves by how deeply they care?

The answer is an exploration of theatrical storytelling that makes an audience buy into a story and care about the characters. To do this, however, you'll need to know—or review—the structure and function of a story, and what makes your particular story *great*.

## THE STRUCTURE OF A STORY | CORRELATION: THE LESSON

This may sound familiar: you create a plan for the day's lesson. It involves a brief lecture, maybe twenty to thirty minutes, and you write something on the board and explain it while the students take notes. You've been to plenty of mandatory training sessions where people explain the importance of breaking up a lesson. Teach for twenty minutes, they say. Change the routine. Give an assignment. A reading. Let them work on the assignment for twenty minutes.

Try another lecture or assignment to hold the attention of every person in the room for the duration of the hour.

The problem, though, is the students are onto you. Many of them are thinking, *If I can just make it through this lecture, he'll give group work and I can talk to my friend about the movie I saw last night*. However, if you transform your lesson into a story, even if it's divided into parts and subroutines and assignments and readings and worksheets, you can engage your students more deeply. You simply have to plan the structure before you tell the story.

Fortunately, every story you've ever enjoyed more or less goes the same way. When we engage with good stories, we're hanging on every word, holding our breath as we turn the page, or not daring to turn our eyes away from the screen or the stage. Telling a good story is a magic trick, one with parts that are easy to learn and use, and even when we know about the parts, we're still filled with wonder at its whole. Imagine what the audience must feel.

Most great stories follow the same simple structure:

1. An Event, or an Inciting Incident that makes the hero need to go on the journey.

- In *The Lord of the Rings*, Sauron launches an offensive to take over the world, Gandalf goes to the Shire to get the one object that could help Sauron succeed, he asks for volunteers to destroy the ring or the world itself will be destroyed, and the heroes reluctantly say yes.

2. The Hero's Journey, where heroes overcome some obstacles, fall to others, and learn about themselves and the world and become better along the way.

- In *Rings*, hijinks and war ensue, but our heroes fight their way through every obstacle, from Gollum to a giant spider to Mordor itself. Their bond is strengthened, and their army grows stronger, even through failures.

3. Climax, where the hero concludes the journey by overcoming the final obstacle.

- The One Ring is destroyed, and there's celebration.

4. Falling Action, where the hero and other characters take an opportunity to see the world anew and reflect on the many changes.

- The destruction of the Ring is not without cost to our characters and the world. Frodo can't quite overcome the way war has changed him and must join the elves and disappear forever.

Audiences love great stories because the structure follows these basic rules. (Even *Avengers: Infinity War* follows them, as surprising as the results are.) Yet too often we provide our own audience—our classroom of students—with a lecture that doesn't even attempt to begin the journey. A central problem with most lectures is they don't always get our audience to care, to enjoy, and to lean in. We hope they'll connect, just as we *expect* our students to listen and take notes. If they don't, it might be because we haven't done anything specific to create a story arc in the lesson.

When we direct actors, we never tell them their objective. We start with questions: "What do you need? Why do you need it?" and "What are you going to do to get it?" These questions spark their curiosity for different choices, exploring the nuances of their character and their story. They have agency over their process and a personal investment in its outcome. They *need* to know, so they go on a journey to make discoveries. Our students, sitting in their desks, pens in hand, also have this need. They could use a little incentive.

Think about a favorite story of yours. What's the inciting incident? Who's the hero? What obstacles do they overcome? What is it about the story that draws you in every single time, that makes you pick that book up again, or watch the film once more? Imagine if you applied that structure to your course. Laying down those breadcrumbs will make the students want to follow you into the woods of literary analysis, organic chemistry, or philosophy.

## THE LESSON AS STORY

### The Inciting Incident

*Teaching Correlation: Motivate Students with a Goal*

You could provide the answer to a question or introduce a new topic by writing it on the board and telling students, "This will be on the test so you better know it." But this would only reaffirm the dividing line. "I have the information you need, and if you want to hear it, you're going to have to listen." Us vs. Them.

Or you can ignite their curiosity. What will happen in your classroom that will make your students *need* to know the answer to today's lesson? If the answer is "it'll be on the final" or "the essay is due on Thursday," that's pretty low stakes—a boring story that's been told far too many times. So how do you make it interesting and entice the students to want to hear it?

*Establish a Goal*

Think of the goal of the day, the lesson to be passed on to the student, as the story. Why do they need to know this? Refer to chapter 2's "Personal Analysis" section: What do I want/need from the students? What potential blocks are in my way? And what can I do to address them? What are the stakes? What is the inciting incident of the day's lesson? Present the day's goal as a motivational force; incite them to acquire the information they'll need for this journey, and send them on that journey as quickly as you can. Examples:

- You announce that next week the students are going to have to calculate a complicated mathematical equation on a test; your announcement is the inciting incident.
  - The test counts for 20 percent of the grade for the class: high stakes. Give them the information they need for the story you're beginning together, a few minutes spent writing the equation on the board.
  - You then break up the formula into smaller sections and divide the students into groups, setting them forth on their hero's journey, with each group assigned a different section of the equation.
  - After preparing for their section, each group needs to teach the others how to do their part, guiding one another on their journey. You've invested them in the story and given them a need to know the information: "I'm going to need to teach my classmates so we can all succeed together."
- The fall of the South in the Civil War changed the social and economic structure of the entire country. You assign your students a paper in which they explore *how* this event connects to the civil rights movement of the 1960s. To spark their journey, each student, or each group, must research a different aspect and piece the correlating events into a timeline, demonstrating how the series of events come together. Once they understand this correlation, can they connect those events to how the Civil Rights Act of 1968 affects their lives today? A personal investment—the need to know—motivates them to set out on this journey.
- Your students need to understand how to craft an introduction paragraph if they're going to write the full essay in a few weeks. You incite their action when you distribute an example that is all wrong: a poorly written thesis statement, with dull sentences and grammar mistakes. Tell them they'll need to figure out what's wrong with this paragraph before they'll ever be

able to write their own. They're united in scorn at the awful sample you've shown them, with a need to rise above it. They want to avoid the Fate of the Scorned Paragraph, which inspires them to invest more deeply in their essays.

We only imagine ourselves in a story if we (a) are invested in the outcome, (b) want to be a part of it, and (c) see something relevant about ourselves reflected in the story—something we would like to imagine ourselves to be. *Our potential.*

## The Hero's Journey

*Teaching Correlation: Giving Students Ownership of Your Lesson*

Now that the students have a need to accomplish their goal, they set out on the journey, mounting a series of difficult steps to meet objectives, learn a little something, and take that knowledge to the next challenge. Like Gandalf in *The Lord of the Rings*, you get to serve as their guide.

You won't do it for them (the equivalent of a lecture in which you give them all the answers and assume they'll just write it all down because that's what you did, and the way they oughta do it now!). But you *will* set out on the journey with them, and how you get them to follow you is as important as the material and information you're giving them. An example:

- You continue to teach your lesson on the format of the essay, in which the end goal of the semester is a five-paragraph paper. Today's goal, then, is to teach them to write a thesis statement. Ask them to tell a story about how they can get something they want:

  - How will you get the keys to your parents' car when you've been grounded for a week? Or how will you convince your boyfriend to go out with you for sushi when he hates it?

- More than likely, their responses will deal with (1) reasons they will achieve their goal and (2) tactics indicating how they will achieve the goal.

  - Next, guide them in phrasing their reasons as a thesis statement. "I deserve the keys because I learned my lesson the previous week and my grades have improved."
  - Encourage them to discuss tactics they will use to prove the reasons are true. "Here's a test I took this week. I got an A. I got that A because I

studied with my friend John. I'm meeting John at the library and then we're going out."
- Point out they can use the same techniques in writing a persuasive essay.

Instead of planning a lecture, then, you're planning questions and ways to guide them to the answers they'll need to step forward. Students will realize that the information was already somewhere inside them, and by drawing their attention to the objectives/actions they used, they prove they have the ability and wherewithal to address the lesson at hand. This gives them ownership over their learning process and builds confidence they'll need going forward.

Your students are now invested, in an organic way, in the first steps of writing a persuasive essay, *and* they now know what a thesis statement is. They'll do better work because they've created an interesting story from their own lives, a practical example that helps them understand structure.

## *Directions for the Journey: A Note on Notes*

If giving students agency over their journey through the lesson is ensuring they set off in the right direction, then note taking is how those students prepare those directions to guarantee they have what they need to continue. This process of organic discovery will benefit the notes students take. With confidence, understanding, and ownership, they'll choose what to write down, recording important pieces of information they'll use later on in the journey. They might even begin to write down observations, ideas they want to bring to class discussions, questions for you or other students, and any number of points about the journey you're guiding them along.

It doesn't hurt to, on occasion, suggest specific points they can include in their notes. Even when another student raises an interesting point or question, try a not-so-subtle "write that down, everyone." This also gives an encouraging ego boost to the student whose comment became a note, even inspiring others to want to have their comments made noteworthy. This will be another part of your journey together, another piece of knowledge you're teaching them.

## *Side Note on "A Note on Notes"*

In theater, when rehearsals become run-throughs of the play (when the actors perform the entire play as if there were an audience), the director takes, and then gives, supportive, guiding notes to the actors. They're points of improvement for performance and blocking, adjustments to moments throughout the play, or additional questions about choices and actions. Actors often have questions about the note. "What did you mean?" or "Can you clarify?" or "What if I try this?" Because the actor is invested in the play, how does the note help the actor, their scene partner, the ensemble, and the production?

Without an impending performance before an audience, what can help a student remember and integrate a note? Just as a bland lecture won't invest students in the material, neither will bland notes.

Notes can be funny: writing on the board "Wath out 4 typos and never use numbrs 4 letters in yor paper" or "Logarithms: How to Be Interesting at Parties." They can be intriguing and lead students to ask questions: "How the Guillotine Saved Democracy." But if they become uninteresting headings followed by thirty minutes of explanation and additional headings, you've already lost them.

Where the actor is engrossed in the note-related discussion and its impact, so too should a student be engrossed in how those notes will matter going forward. The student should ask, "How does the note help me better absorb and retain the subject matter? How does it help my classmates and my ability to interact with them on the subject, and my ability to navigate the course?" Instead, students often want to know if what they're writing down will be on the test.

They'll get a far more intrinsic understanding of the notes if you relate it to previous material. This could be text readings, contributions they made to the class discussion, how they might be able to apply the notes to their lives and their assignments, and hints about how these notes may affect the story going forward. Finding ways to make notes matter to students will get them to connect new information with old in a much more organic, direct way.

## Obstacles to the Hero's Journey

*Teaching Correlation: How to Help Our Students through the Hard Parts*

Sometimes students face difficulties on their journey in our classes. A low grade on a quiz demotivates them. They feel embarrassed about being wrong in a class discussion. How can we guide students toward meeting these obstacles, giving them what they need to learn from the struggle and overcome them?

To paraphrase Yoda, failure is a great lesson.

In rehearsals, actors need to know they can and will fail. And not only is "failure" an important part of their process but also failure itself becomes redefined with each new attempt as their confidence grows with every risk they take. If the response to each "failure" is "We need to fail at times in order to learn; try again," then each risk will be greater and the results will be more rewarding for the actor, the ensemble, and the audience.

As you impart this lesson-as-story, what task can you plan for them that makes sure they take risks, and perhaps even gives them a chance to fail and also *learn* from that failure and try again? Examples:

- In a history class, you tell students that for an upcoming test (inciting incident), they'll have to label a timeline of events (objective) based on the correlating chapter reading: The Beginning and End of Prohibition, Causes of World War II, or Nixon's Impeachment (obstacles).

  - Ask for volunteers to mark up a timeline of important events connected to the lesson. You're prepared with the "right" answers, but in the lesson, only give them certain key points and have them fill in what's missing. Ask them to teach *you* the lesson as a journey. What's the inciting incident? Who is the protagonist of this story (the Allies in World War II, for instance)? The students are now needed by their team to complete the timeline, reinforcing their part in the lesson (the story) and in themselves.
  - Next, let them fail. They'll forget an important step or mislabel a historical event. Let them work together to correct it. "Take another look at the step you labeled as the Watergate break-in. You have the next step as impeachment discussions. Are you forgetting something? Maybe a couple of reporters?" Someone in the group shouts out "Woodward and Bernstein!" Another student adds that step to the timeline, while another student asks, "What did they do?" A third student calls out an answer. The students *want* to add details.
  - You and your students are making discoveries to get the information they need, and they're discovering that the reward for a wrong answer is the chance to discover the right one together.

- In an English class:

  - Inciting incident: Assign an essay. Plan a lesson in which you outline an essay on the board, in specific detail, from introduction to conclusion. But you only write down what the students say, setting them off on their journey.
  - Obstacles: At the end, ask what steps did they miss? Why? How could they fix the missing pieces in time for writing a draft? This reinforces that every first draft is full of mistakes or omissions, and that's okay. You give them Permission to Screw Up (see chapter 6). Now how can they fix it? This teaches them there's always something they can improve or make stronger; it just takes additional

effort to get there. You're giving them a process they'll need later in the journey, when they face these obstacles alone in their room, staring at a computer screen.

- In math:

  - Inciting incident: Suggest to the students that there's been a decrease in the ability of people to use reason to solve problems in everyday life. Maybe pull a recent news story that illustrates someone making a mistake due to lack of reason or problem solving skills. Explain that the ability to solve these problems will help them avoid the consequences this news story discusses.
  - Obstacles: Ask the students to create word problems for other students to solve.
  - Hero's journey: The word problems give them ownership of their journey instead of bringing in word problems of your own. Jane has twice the number of oranges as Bob but one-third the number of oranges as Mary. Have them put the word problem on the board, and ask another student to solve it. By letting students create *and* overcome obstacles, you help them find flaws in the understanding of the initial problem, as well as its answer.

Throughout all of it, you're asking students to join you in front of the others, to perform, to collaborate in the telling of this story, and they're motivated not just by the fear of performance in front of the room but also by the *need* to understand the material up to this point.

And what happens when they screw up? How can you address their mistakes and ensure they still have agency and ownership over their journey?

- Treat their mistakes as obstacles they're capable of overcoming, and remind them you and the whole class will support and guide them in their efforts. When they make a mistake, treat it as a beginning of a larger discussion—a learning experience.
- "I didn't do the homework." "Why?" "I read the chapter too quickly." "What's a better way to read?" "I thought I got this, but it's clear I don't." "What made you stop when you realized it wasn't clear to you? What got in your way of asking for help? Why pretend to understand?"

This can open a larger life question: why do we fear being wrong, being different, and being left out? If we can bring our students to a better personal understanding of those issues in their lives, then we're helping them with study habits, test-taking skills, and specific course outcomes. We're arming them with tactics they can use to navigate greater journeys beyond that of a student: careers, relationships, hobbies, and goals.

## The Climax

*Teaching Correlation: Assessing Your Students*

There comes a time when you have to leave your students to fight their greatest battle, putting knowledge into practice on their own. Gandalf fell down the chasm, leaving the hobbits to continue their journey alone. You assign homework. You pass out the test. Now let them guide themselves on their individual journeys through what might be the hardest part. As guide and storyteller, you get to decide what the final battle will be and how it might best measure whether your students have gained the knowledge and understanding they need to move forward.

Just as notes on the board and an accompanying lecture might seem like the easy answer to "how do I communicate this information," sometimes we might decide a test or a paper is the easiest answer to the question "How do I assess whether they've learned what they need to know to move forward?" What other assessment techniques might there be that can serve as challenging, engaging assignments that still require students to prove that they've come out of this week/module/course with what they need to succeed?

- Instead of assessing students' knowledge of the parts of a flower with a multiple-choice test, bring in a flower (real or otherwise) and have them tape Post-it labels to the accurate parts. Especially when using a fake flower, you can have them stick notes to the petals, the stem, and the stigma to demonstrate their understanding. (It might make for a challenging trip back to the office, but the real-world application is a much better story for them to tell you than picking—and often guessing—the right answer on a Scantron sheet.)
- At some point in their writing course, students are going to have to compose that persuasive essay. They can discuss their personal experiences writing the paper: have them include a paragraph on the last page in which they explain their writing process. Encourage them to include fun personal stories: "My mom made me come downstairs for dinner just when I was on a roll." "My little brother wanted me to stop and help him with *his* homework."
- When you have your students give their informative speech, rearrange the classroom so they're speaking in the round, surrounded by the energy of support and encouragement. Include a Q&A as part of the assignment so their fellow students can help them communicate all the information of the

speech by asking follow-up questions, guiding them to areas that might need further elaboration.

Because you have arranged a climax to a story they'll be invested in, they get to tell that story themselves instead of just reading from pages in a notebook the night before the big test. They prove to you that they have absorbed the story and its "moral," and they prove to themselves they understand and have ownership of these new skills—and that they're able to tell this story themselves down the line, without the support of Gandalf.

**Falling Action**

*Teaching Correlation: Giving More than Just a Grade*

What happens after the final battle? When you return the papers or tests or discuss the speeches, plan on guiding them through the nuances of success. They all did well. They all learned something! Maybe all the students did well on a particular section of a test or the whole class improved on compelling introductions to their speeches or they successfully solved a particularly challenging mathematical equation.

In your discussion of the climax assignment, ask them for one area they were afraid of *and* feel they are particularly happy with how they conquered it. It could be as simple as a hard question they got right or a discovery they made in the midst of a test. Congratulate them so they're reminded of this success as you take the next leg of this overall journey to accomplish their objective.

But what if they fail? What if they don't do well—they miss an important series of questions or screw up the thesis statement? Too often we assume they'll realize what they've done and look over it or come to us for extra help.

The reality is that they usually look at the grade and have some sort of visceral reaction. "A 62? But I studied for three hours!" "C? But I did three drafts!" Teach them how to overcome failure, to embrace it as a necessary part of learning. Show them how to not only climb out of the hole and continue on the journey but also ensure they have what they need to succeed at the next attempt. Ask them, "If you could tell this part of the story again, what would you do differently?"

"There were way more formulas than I thought. I'd study a few nights earlier." "I would have spoken up with my question during the timeline exercise. I forgot an entire decade." "I wouldn't have let that fight with my best friend distract me from dissecting the pig in lab."

The analysis of successes and failures in the test, paper, presentation, group project, or speech is one last opportunity for your students to learn how human they really are. Try not to let the pressure of time cause you to shrug off the collective grades and move on to the next module or unit. We have a schedule to keep, after all, but taking the extra time now to give this important lesson will lead the students into the next leg of their journey prepared, bolstered, and inspired rather than demoralized by a poor performance on a test. They'll be ready to take this failure and apply what they've learned to conquering the next obstacle on their journey.

## TRUSTING THE PLAN — AND YOURSELF — IN THE CLASSROOM

How can you be sure your students will respond to this storytelling technique? You've been using the same lectures and techniques for so long and have been giving the same test for years. What will happen if you change? Or maybe, while reading this chapter, you discovered you've been using some of these techniques already, but you're uneasy about taking the leap and committing to lesson-as-story. How can you be sure it will work?

Trust and risk.

The same way that you're working to establish an environment in which your students need to feel comfortable taking risks, in which they're trusting you and their fellow students, you need to flourish in this environment as well. Trust *yourself*. Trust your lesson plan, your expertise, and your abilities as an educator to guide you through these exercises. Know that it grows stronger and clearer with the *doing* of it. Prepare yourself, and prepare the lesson.

And the students? Trust your students to engage in the lesson you prepare for them. What if you try something and it doesn't work? Failure is a great teacher, even for educators, and there's always tomorrow. The journey you're taking together will include plenty of opportunities to adjust and play. A teacher's lesson is the same way. You trust yourself and your students, and you play. You try things. You make adjustments. You're there with them, trying out these choices.

### Mike

I was directing at a college where the students in the play were a combination of actors-in-training for the drama program and students who just liked to act. Some had been doing it since elementary school and were very good, but their career outlook had guided them toward physics or accounting or nursing. The mandate from the college was to cast as many as possible and be as inclusive as possible, which set up a conundrum: I'd need to direct some students who were being trained in the art of acting as collaborative storytellers and some who were just there for fun.

*"I'm pretty sure I'm ready for this,"* I thought. I used to teach general education classes such as composition and public speaking, where I'd have some students who were majors in the topic, some who were far better at math than English, and some who had struggled throughout their entire academic careers all gathered in one classroom. I knew how to adjust a lesson to meet these different majors, and also different learning styles, ages, cultures, and past experiences, and an allotment of variety that makes every lesson a challenge to get across to everyone involved. In this new drama program, what could go wrong?

I started by making sure rehearsals were fun, creative, and yes, collaborative. I gave the English major an acting adjustment by making a Charles Dickens reference. "You should try harder to get her to go with you. You sound like Oliver asking for more, and we all know how that turned out." For the math major, I got a bit more logical. "What will you discover if you get her to go with you? What's the benefit? What are the odds of her saying yes if you try it this way?"

For the student who had never done theater before, I spent a little time encouraging her to ask questions, and setting up an environment in which she trusted—and was trusted by—everyone else in the ensemble. Rehearsing with the students was going well!

What I didn't expect in this college theater were adult professionals who didn't know some basic rules of rehearsals. The head of publicity wanted to show up randomly and stop rehearsals so he could take pictures and film for the theater department's website. This would violate every attempt I'd make at establishing a safe space where students could take risks and fail, where the entire rule was "no one will see this except us, so you might as well try!" The costume designer had no interest in a collaborative space and didn't want to take any feedback from me or the actors. The set designer didn't even want to have a conversation about basic ideas.

Throughout all of this, I had to find positive, noninvasive ways to change the way things were done at this theater—the way they'd always been done—so that the story being told would work in the way I knew it could. Through working together, we changed the way things had always been done. But not without a little confusion, some slightly hurt feelings, and a number of meetings.

In the end, the show was better than it otherwise would have been. The students became an ensemble and gave great performances. Sometimes, people just need to see the results of collaborative storytelling.

The resistance in educational institutions can be great. "You're doing *what* in Algebra II?" And just as in theater, the outcome will be worth it.

## The Story of Schedules: Telling Stories Well . . . and *Fast*!

There's pressure in rehearsal, much as there's pressure in a classroom. You have a lot to accomplish and very little time to get there. You might have to work around actor conflicts, holidays, and available rehearsal space, while in the classroom you're also working with holidays, short days, snow days, and quarter, term, and semester end dates.

And in a rehearsal, sometimes a scene isn't working. The actors are trying, but something isn't right. Instead of continuing to run the scene, or moving on, you try something. You give the actors an improv exercise related to the scene and use it to help an actor better connect to their acting partner. The time spent playing with them in this way accomplishes so much more than running the scene again ever would. Your next rehearsal will run more smoothly, and accomplish a lot more, because you took the time to play, you trusted the actors, and they trusted you.

When class time is short and yet you *have* to test the students tomorrow, let them create their *own Jeopardy* questions about a class topic to foster a close reading of the material. This helps them understand the lesson, and it lets them know what and how to study and why it matters. Games like this will engage your students and fill your classroom with energy, enthusiasm, understanding, and fun.

You can also play story games to encourage students to tell the story of the lesson in their own words. This is the one surefire way to make certain you understand a topic—to be able to explain it to someone else in your own words. For examples of storytelling exercises you can run in the classroom, see appendix J for *Three-Headed Alien* and appendix H for *One-Word-at-a-Time Storytelling* and *Storytelling Chorus*. Right now, it might feel as if that would take up too much time, but the value of the students' agency over the material and investment in its outcome will foster greater—and faster—student understanding.

## THE JOURNEY BEGINS

When you present the lesson as a story, it works because stories have worked on humans for thousands of years. We've told stories with cave paintings, runes, and religious texts, all used to teach one another how to get done what we've all agreed—collaboratively—we need to do. Giving students the need to take that first step in the story is imperative, and once you erase the division between students and content that's created by "because I said so" and nurture their need for this material, everything else you do is just good storytelling.

You'll inspire the students to *need* to know what happens next. Thanos has wiped out half of the entire universe, gobsmacking the audience and their expectations in the process. For the Avengers, the result was a sequel—*Avengers: Endgame*—to which audiences flocked on opening weekend, desperate to know what happens next. It became one of the highest-grossing movies ever made. Imagine what storytelling like this can do for your students.

Now, imagine your ideal setting for the telling of this story: A campfire? A raised platform? What if you don't have those ideal conditions? What surrounds you that could help you take the story even further into the depths of their imaginations and minds?

*Chapter Four*

# All of Your Classroom *Is* a Stage

The great thing about telling stories around a campfire is that you aren't occupying a physical space that identifies you as a leader. You're part of a group of shared storytellers leading and following one another on these journeys in the dark. Everyone around the fire is deeply affected by the surrounding darkness and strange noises just outside the flickering light.

Good storytellers recognize that *where* you tell a story can affect *how* you tell a story. They can use all the elements of the environment to give context to the events of the story they're telling. Weaving together an imaginative and visual atmosphere draws the listeners in and connects them to the story, to you, and to each other.

In a perfect world, we would get to teach in environments that inspire and support the story we're trying to tell. People experience strong emotional responses to environments and recognize immediately when a place feels homey and warm or mysterious and spooky. All the wonderful preparation and perspective discussed in earlier chapters may run smack into the physical and psychological challenges of the physical space.

Most of us teach on perfectly nice, sometimes lovely campuses, in perfectly functional spaces, but sometimes they're not so nice. Even if we teach in a beautiful, clean technological marvel of a classroom in a gorgeous building, the environment won't do the trick all by itself. Gathering folks in dark woods is a good start for ghost stories, but how we relate to those dark woods—and how those trees and their gnarly, spidery branches add to the story—is what brings it to roaring (or screaming) life. Environments give feelings and create expectations.

Most students enter a classroom expecting the tradition of a real or imagined dividing line: the concept of a *front of room* and *back of room*. The age-old classroom design many of us have grown accustomed to creates a void: Us vs. Them. We can't consider the front of the room, or the back, or wherever the teacher is standing, sitting, or moving, as the stage.

Instead, what if the entire classroom *was* the stage, all of us sharing that space and using it to teach and learn? By moving throughout the space together and physically and dynamically activating the lessons, we create a different environment, one in which our students should feel motivated to speak and stand, and make choices and take risks like an actor. Whether the gap is visual or psychological, we can empower our students to bridge it and to believe in their ability to do so.

The job of the actor is to inspire the audience to cross the gap between the auditorium and the stage and enter the story that's being told, with the actor as the shaman or guide. How the performers treat the physical space they occupy with the audience is critical. Everyone is an essential part of this story being told in this room at this moment in time, and everyone needs to be connected to this story, whether they're in the front row or the balcony.

## WHAT'S YOUR STAGE? TRANSFORMING THE ENVIRONMENT

What role does the environment play in your ability to inspire your students to cross that gap? What's your relationship to the rooms that you teach in, and how do you adjust when you're working in optimal or challenging conditions? Are you in a room where you have adequate space, light, heat and AC, and up-to-date equipment, and where the walls and ceiling are in good condition? To create your shared stage, start with how you relate to the space.

When a theater director begins a project, the initial space never, ever looks or feels like the eventual stage that the actors will perform on. To help the actors visualize the eventual performance space, the director works with stage managers so they can "translate" the set design by taping the outlines of the set (walls and staircases) on the rehearsal studio floor. They add rehearsal furniture, and actors are given physical props. This allows the creative team to gradually cross the gap from a rehearsal room to a fully realized visual world of the play weeks later.

Likewise, you've prepared for your class for weeks, possibly months. You know the story of this class better than anyone, and the type of environment that would most dynamically support your students. So how do you transform your blank "rehearsal room" into the fully realized world you'll use to collaborate with your students and tell the story of your class?

- On day 1, arrive early; get to know this room, and infuse it with the energy you want it to have. Take out the trash, and make sure the equipment works. Set the stage.

- Walk around in the space. Even if it's a room you feel you know well, spend time examining every detail, and don't gloss over the windows, ceiling, or floor. What's different since the last time you taught in here? How are *you* different since then?
- If the room is new to you, take as much time as possible to walk every inch of it, and notice everything. What color are the walls? Is it hot? Cool? What kind of energy do you feel when you walk in? Do you have a desk? Where is it, and would you like to move it? Can the student chairs be moved? What can you use in here to enhance the story?
- If you had to create a story inspired by this space, what kind of story would it be? If it's a ghost story, remember how fun and compelling ghost stories can be!
- If a game were going to be played in this room, what type of game would it best be suited for? *Jeopardy*? Hide and seek?

Be honest about the feeling that the room has, whether that supports your goals for this class or it's something you'd like to change. Getting to know the room with this richness of detail will help you answer the question "what is available to me?" You wouldn't overlook your relationship with the students, so why would you overlook your relationship to the physical environment, or home, you'll be working together in for the next ten to fifteen weeks?

## PREPARING YOURSELF TO TRANSFORM THE ENVIRONMENT

There are many options to ensure the students engage with, and vividly remember, the material you're teaching. Physical gestures and movement can be evocative and memorable. How you occupy the space physically is just as important. You don't need to choreograph every physical moment of your class, but you can create a physical outline, and you'll be able to confidently improvise movements between key moments.

This will also make you aware of your distinctive, habitual gestures. Every one of us has them, and our personal gestures are akin to our regional dialects; they make us uniquely who we are. We need to be flexible enough to neutralize them (gestures that are constantly repeated lose their power over time), enhance them, or develop new ones. Working with specific descriptors/actions and a movement vocabulary can help you organically discover new physical expression that's rooted in intentional use.

The "Physical Preparation and Physical Storytelling for the Teacher" section of chapter 2 discussed several approaches. Though you can apply any movement technique that works for you, a great example is the Laban Movement Analysis.

## ONE METHOD OF ANALYZING OUR PHYSICAL MOVEMENT (WITHOUT GETTING TOO SELF-CONSCIOUS!)

Laban Movement Analysis can help us understand the difference between how we think we're physically telling a story and how we may *actually* be telling the story. The Laban method focuses on the relationship between body and space, the effort an action takes, and the physical shape that results from that effort. It's a rich and detailed method of movement that takes time and study to become proficient with, but you can begin with its basic concepts to better understand how you're physically communicating.

For now, focus solely on the four categories of Laban movement that connect respectively to space, weight, time, and flow. Even these basics will help you better understand and describe your unique movement characteristics and support you in creating a physical outline to tell the story. The four categories are (1) space: direct/indirect, (2) weight: strong/light, (3) time: quick/sustained, and (4) flow: bound/free.

Select a short portion from your lecture or lesson plan, or a planned introduction to the class or course (three to four minutes in length). Ask a trusted friend to film you, or film yourself, in the privacy of your home. Imagine you're in the classroom, and don't use a mirror (yet!). Even if it's excruciating, watch the video once to get over your own criticisms; now watch it a second time, and include your trusted friend.

What role does movement play in your lesson? Using the Laban scale above, how would you describe your movement? Not "I'm stiff as a board" or "I flap like a chicken," but sticking to the scale, notate the movement you observe. Would you describe it as indirect and bound? Strong and sudden?

For example, if you felt a section was indirect and bound (arms tightly held to your sides; you were slumped a bit), instead of thinking about what to do with your hands, focus on playing the action of being more direct and free. Trust that the content will come alive with your focused action supporting it. Film yourself again, and observe the differences. Try this several times, and focus on a new internal action each time, instead of "I must not slump." What action could *free* you from feeling slumped? How do those changes affect the potency of what you're communicating each time?

Go through your lesson plan/lecture, and score it. Then practice it on your feet with the actions/descriptors you've assigned. If they don't work or don't feel natural, try different ones (for additional movement adjectives, see appendix O). You'll experience the difference in how connected you feel physically and psychologically to your intention, and how confident you feel in your body.

## STUDENTS ENTER THE STAGE

Now you'll need students prepared to create this shared space with you. If you begin a lecture that starts with "let's get rid of the division between the front of the room and the back," they might become suspicious. In theater rehearsals, the importance of discovery lies in organic exploration. You need your students to *want* to become your partner in psychologically and physically transforming the classroom into a stage, and they need to discover it for themselves.

The dictionary definition of improvisation is "making do with what's at hand." Actors can transform a crummy acting studio with leaky ceilings and plaster bits crunching on the floor into a creative space that produces interstellar travel, alien worlds, or natural disasters. Actors accept the environment they're in and ask, "What *could* it be?"

Students in an English class reading *The Count of Monte Cristo* become the prisoners working together to escape their jail, or in chemistry class, students must determine what acidic compound might get that stain out of the wall. In other words, use the environment itself as an obstacle the class must overcome together to achieve the next step on their journey, to focus on the power of what *is* available instead of worrying about what *isn't* available. One empowers the occupants of the environment, while the latter makes everyone simply wish they were somewhere else.

The following exercises are great for warm-ups or icebreakers, but they can also be used during the semester to transform the student's physical experience into an open, expressive one. That expression will begin to show itself in more "traditional" classroom activities: students will take better notes, make eye contact during lectures, and respond to others' ideas in class discussions. They'll connect to the discoveries of learning because they're not distracted by shortcomings of the space, or surrendering to the physical separation of more traditional classrooms.

## EXERCISES TO TRANSFORM ANY CLASSROOM

For full descriptions and variations of the following exercises, see the appendices.

### *Zing* (Appendix M)

*The What*

If there's room enough to move desks and tables out of the way, stand the group in a circle. One student starts with the word "Zing" and gestures and makes eye contact with another student and they pass Zing—and its connected energy—on. Like hot potato, when one student gets Zing, they pass it to any other student in the circle as soon as possible. After a time, instruct them "side to side only," meaning they can only pass to students on their left and right, and then "all the way around," at which time they pass it in the same direction all the way around as many times as you want.

*The Why*

To activate the learning environment. Too often students get comfortable and, yes, lazy in their desks with their notes and phones and drifting thoughts. Getting them on their feet combines your area and theirs into a playing space both active and energized. It gets the students moving and increases their awareness and attention. Yes And reinforces there's nothing they can say or do that's wrong. Being present and connected to you and one another is rewarded.

## *What Are You Doing?* (Appendix L)

*The What*

The students stand in two lines, single file, and the first person in each line—for our purposes, Jerry and George—are facing one another. Jerry asks George, "What are you doing?" George replies with the first idea that pops into his mind: "Eating an apple." Jerry begins to physically perform *eating an apple* while George moves to the back of his line. The student behind George, Elaine, steps forward and asks Jerry, "What are you doing?" Jerry replies with the first idea that he has: "Riding a bike," stops doing his own movement, and moves to the back of his line while Elaine performs *riding a bike*. And so on.

Encourage the students to wait until the exact moment they're asked "what are you doing?" to come up with an answer. If they can get themselves to be *present*, not planning, and taking in the "performances," they will be inspired by *everything* that has come before their turn, not simply what comes *immediately* before it. The exercise will help them to trust their impulses and get over the fear of what happens when they participate, when they're asked a question they don't know, or when they draw a blank.

*The Why*

We've all experienced a time as kids in school in which the teacher announces, "Today, we're going to read chapter 5 together." He divides up the chapter into paragraphs, one for each student, and while the first student reads, the rest of the class ignores her, desperately counting to their respective paragraph and making sure there's nothing in it that could cause embarrassment: a mispronounced word, an uncomfortable pause, or an overly long sentence. The students, then, ignore every other paragraph except their own and miss the entire point of the lesson.

As Keith Johnson notes, they're not *listening*. They want to hide—from the teacher, from each other, from the textbook, and from anyone except the voice in their head repeating, *Don't mess this up*. And once they get used to not listening, how easy does it become for them to disappear into a device? This exercise encourages acting on impulse, trusting, and conquering the fear that goes along with the classroom. And no hiding!

## *Blind Offers* (Keith Johnstone, *Impro*; Appendix A)

*The What*

This exercise works best in your second or third week, after the students have become more comfortable with the space, with you, and with one another. Ask two students to face each other: Sam and Al. Sam goes first. He makes a silent, physical offer to Al in the form of a still pose that is held. The pose can be representative of an action, such as tying a shoe, or an abstract gesture with arms akimbo.

Sam picks arms out, mid-flap, like a giant eagle. Al responds with a pose of his own, one inspired by Sam's offer or an impulse-driven response. Al drops to one knee and opens his arms in an embrace, as if waiting and worshipping Sam's eagle-like pose. While Al and Sam are both holding their poses, Sam then replies with "thank you," at which time both students go back to a neutral stance. Sam then repeats the exercise two more times, and they switch, allowing Al the opportunity to make three offers (three silent, physical poses) and thank Sam for his response.

*The Why*

So many students *hate* participating. If they're required to give an oral report, they'll read it from a page without inflection or personality, not daring to reveal even an ounce of themselves. If they're asked a question to which they don't know the answer, they'll stare back in horror, hoping the instructor will move on, maybe forget they exist, or they're willing to let the silence stretch until time's up and the class ends.

*Blind Offers* is almost wordless, which helps, but it's also a reminder that they're not alone, that they're in this class with others they can trust, and that they can support one another. Since every offer will be responded to in some way, it reinforces the idea that every offer will be accepted and no idea will be rejected, and that's what builds the trust. And the reward for participation, regardless of the attempt, should be gratitude. It's also great for tight places since it involves two volunteers at a time.

For any of these activities, ending them with a discussion of observations is a great way to focus these discoveries. "What did you notice about yourself?" is an excellent beginning. By getting students to make observations about their own behavior, bodies, and energy, they may notice (1) the dramatic differences in how they feel about the classroom, themselves, their classmates, their teacher, and the subject matter and (2) how disconnected they so often are in a classroom in which they're in a desk, staring at their phones, and barely connected to anyone else.

## WELCOMING YOUR STUDENTS INTO A SPACE WITH INADEQUATE BASICS

**Rose**

When our theater department was receiving an external evaluation, I was charged with escorting the two evaluators to a few of our "lesser" classrooms, particularly to the infamous "Room 052." (I think every school has a version of this room.) It was located in a sub-basement; the few windows were tiny, and all you could see out of them was a concrete walkway. Dark green Formica tiles covered the floor like a kitchen from the 1950s, and the tiles hadn't been fixed or replaced since the '50s either.

It flooded regularly, so there were water stains on the cinder block walls, and the air smelled vaguely like an abandoned secondhand book shop. The rehearsal furniture in this room were pieces that the nicer classrooms rejected: three-legged tables, wobbly chairs, and ragged wooden cubes that no student wanted to sit on for fear of getting splinters in their behinds.

There was also a locked door that no one had the key to, and in all the years I taught in that room, I never saw it open; no one knew what was inside. That door really creeped me out. Room 052 was also where all Intro to Acting classes were scheduled. Leadership's theory was we needed to save the better classrooms for the theater majors. My worry was "we won't *get* any theater majors if this is their introduction to the major." It was a testament to every intro teacher and their transformative abilities that we had a healthy theater program for so long.

So when I brought the external evaluators into room 052, I simply said, "And this is our Intro to Acting classroom." There was a beat of silence, and one evaluator finally said, "I saw a room like this once. Thirty years ago when I was in the Soviet bloc before the Berlin Wall came down."

There are legendarily awful rehearsal spaces that theater folk will talk about. During a recent gathering of actors, after a pint (or two) the conversation turned to a "biggest rat you ever saw in a theater" competition. Those are funny stories in retrospect, but what actors remember most is how they collectively transformed the space.

One of the most common reasons that teachers lose heart and passion for their work is being asked to teach in difficult environments. It's hard to feel respected when you're asked to teach in a room that has questionable heat, with a peeling ceiling that sends bits down after a rainstorm, windows that don't close/open, or worse, a room with absolutely no air flowing.

It's easy to see how this space would have negative energy, and easy to see how a teacher starts to imagine the unseen Powers of the Administration who assign inadequate rooms. (That fantasy usually extends to imagining the Administrators in a mansion surrounded by light and munching bonbons, on chairs with four good legs.) A 2018 study found direct links between teachers who reported unsatisfactory working conditions and attrition rate (Geiger 2018). Students will acutely feel *your* energy, especially on a first day. They're already on high alert: a new class, a new instructor, and a new room (or a room known for being too cold or too spooky).

What's within your power to change in the space to create a safe and supportive environment, even before the students arrive? Think about the episode of *Friends* where Ross was getting married—for the second time (don't think about how that marriage ended up; just stay with us for a minute). Emily the bride wanted their ceremony in the old church where her parents had married, and when they found it had been torn down and reduced to a pile of rubble, they initially fought because she wanted to postpone the wedding, and Ross wanted to change the venue. Both options made them miserable.

Then Ross (with Monica's help, we suspect) had the idea of transforming the space. With a few strings of fairy lights and a flick of the switch, aisles and piles of bricks were transformed into a magical realm of vaulted ceilings and half walls that arced into the night sky. Then, he *offered* that to Emily, empowering her by saying they could make other additions and changes to the space together, and if she still didn't like it, they would figure it out—together. The wedding went forward in that environment, and television history was made.

So, as the leader for a class, if you find yourself in a variation of a torn-down church, you need to get past the inadequacy of the space, or the marriage won't happen. What do you absolutely need for the learning to take place? You've got yourself, your students, and the basic technical equipment that you need: the essentials. Everything else *enhances* that experience, but start with accepting that you have everything you need. What's within your power to change in the space to create a safe and supportive environment, even before the students arrive?

## Collaborative Exercises to Improve Rooms with Inadequate Basics

If you're assigned a room with inadequate basics (leaky ceiling, cracked plaster, and broken chairs), unless they're new freshmen, your students will have been in one or more of those classrooms too. They'll remember having to bundle up on frigid days because of the drafts whistling through the windows, or having to walk past the broken desk that had yellow tape across it so that no one would sit on it, a constant reminder of neglect.

Students will vividly remember those flaws; they'll remember how those flaws weren't addressed by their teacher or the administration. They were expected to handle it without explanation. They'll remember how much money they or their parents paid in tuition, or their impending student loan bill. Most of all, they'll remember how disrespected they felt being assigned to that room.

Your first objective is to inspire the students to accept that they have everything they need to be successful in this class in this room, and that collectively, you can transform the space into one of learning and empowerment in spite of the physical challenges.

### Rose

When my college decided to build a new performing arts center, a few undergrad teachers and I were moved to "transitional" spaces in the old gymnasiums on the far side of campus. My main teaching room had been an old (old) dance studio—no windows, poor air, terrible overhead lights that were constantly "out," chipped wooden floors that gave splinters to anyone who dared to take their shoes off, and so on. The most challenging part was that the room was freezing—absolutely and utterly wear-long-sleeves-and-a-jacket freezing.

I complained to my department, who complained to facilities, who booted it back to someone else in the chain; "they" said the entire building was on a single "setting" and that it wasn't possible to put the heat up for that one room. And that was the answer we got for years. Years. "Nothing to be done. Deal with it." The irony was that the room was coldest during August and September—and it would get tolerably warm by November.

I did my best to accept the shortcomings of the room, involving the students in exercises that would transform the space and get our blood circulating, and I reminded them to bring warm clothing each week. We continued to report the poor conditions. One day, in the middle of one of my improv classes, after a rigorous exercise we paused to discuss discoveries. The room was so cold that within minutes folks started shivering.

Finally, one student—who was wearing the heaviest sweater of all—yelled, "It's so fucking cold! It's SO FUCKING COLD! How the fuck am I supposed to learn anything when all I can think about is how cold I am and how the people I gave my tuition money to don't give a rat's ass about us?" His outburst channeled what we were all feeling: that we were supposed to teach, and learn, in unhealthy conditions. Worse, the students were paying for the privilege of trying to learn in a meat locker.

Instead of chiding him for the outburst, we collectively agreed to adopt the mantra "It's so fucking cold!" for the rest of the class and semester. We did exercises and improvs that integrated the temperature (and poor lighting!), and it helped our attitudes to honestly acknowledge those poor conditions—that the administration couldn't/wouldn't address.

Actors (and theater departments) are, unfortunately, often expected to "make do" because of how resourceful theater people can be and because of the nature of the work. We decided to use our energy to focus on transformation and learning. The class became a powerfully bonded ensemble, and we had a brilliant semester that was filled with discovery, laughter, and some pretty potent mantras!

The following exercises can optimize the physical environment for you and your students, regardless of how challenging the physical classroom itself might be. Each exercise reinforces students' abilities to transform their environment and ensure they will better connect to you, one another, and the lesson at hand, without being distracted by their less-than-satisfactory surroundings.

## Walk and Rename Objects (Keith Johnstone; Appendix K)

*The What*

If space permits, ask the students to silently walk around in the room; encourage them to explore as many aspects of the room as possible. If there isn't room for students to move, have them stand, and slowly turn a full 360 degrees so they can fully take in the space. Make a mental note of who is looking at the floor, who's walking/standing with hunched shoulders, who's fishing for their phone, and who suddenly seems to doubt that they know *how* to walk or stand (shuffling, fidgeting, etc.).

Notice if anyone seems to avoid "the teacher's area" near your desk, or avoids "crossing the gap" of space between the assumed teacher's area and student seating area. Observe how they do or don't share their energy with the room, or each other. Give them a few moments to ground themselves and really look around.

Now, ask them to clearly point to any object in the room, and rename it *out loud* with the first noun that comes to mind; they can call it anything, except what that object *literally* is. For example, a light switch can be renamed a table, a chair is a flower, and a smartboard becomes an iceberg. Students can point to fixtures, floor tiles, or any physical elements of the room. Encourage them to rename as many things as possible.

After a minute or so, have them pause from the verbal renaming but continue to walk around the room. Ask if they notice anything about the room itself. Does it feel smaller or larger? Does it seem to have higher or lower ceilings? If anyone resorted to using proper names (calling items Bob, Meghan, or Kyle), in the second round, guide them to use nouns only for their descriptors. Ask them to start the renaming process again, and give new names for objects they've already "christened." Allow another minute or two for the second round. Eventually call to go to neutral, which means everyone can relax their bodies and the active portion of the exercise is finished.

In the post-exercise discussion, it's not uncommon to hear a student say, "I've been in this room a hundred times, but I've never noticed that chair/light fixture/big dent on the wall." Did they struggle with letting go of the perceived "right" answer? How did it feel when they knew there was no right or wrong but that any offer/word that they gave would be accepted? Did the exercise tap into their fear of Being Wrong, which of course taps into fear of Rejection and fear of Humiliation? What was the worst thing that could happen if they called a desk a reindeer?

Encourage them to try this exercise, verbally or silently, in other environments. It helps them realize they're surrounded by potential sources of inspiration and support, they have the power to transform the simplest thing into an opportunity, and they possess untapped resources that help their learning. Whether it's a science, an English, or an architecture class, this exercise nurtures curiosity and helps students ask "what *could* it be?" which is applicable to all learning.

*The Why*

This exercise helps students be present in their surroundings, expand awareness of their physical environment, strengthen observation skills, and nurture imaginations and their ability to transform what surrounds them. What are the things they walk past every day? How do those surroundings present opportunities?

Too often students isolate themselves at their desks; *Walk and Rename Objects* brings them out of their bubbles and empowers them to claim the space around them. It allows them to take ownership of the new world that they created, helps to erase any physical gaps that exist in the room, and is a strong first step to physically creating a shared space. As a bonus, because it requires commitment to their first word/first thought, it strengthens their ability to commit to an idea and offer it aloud, instead of judging a first thought and stifling it.

## Count to 20

*The What*

If space allows, have students stand in a circle. If not, have them stand where they can see as many of their classmates as possible. The group is going to count to twenty, one person at a time. Any student can start by saying "one," and a different person says the next number, and so on. However, if two people speak at the same time, or overlap even a little, the count goes back to "one." Don't create an order, and if students begin to organically create an order and lock into a pattern ("Wayne said one, Elaine said two, I said three, and I'm sticking to that"), ask them to release that and allow the called-out numbers to be random.

You can do variations of this; you can start with a lower number (one to ten) and, once they've achieved that, build up to a higher goal. Ask students to close their eyes, face away from one another, and observe what does/ doesn't seem to help them focus. Try to give them at least five minutes, and be prepared that students will want to keep doing the exercise until they "get it."

The exercise encourages heightened listening, intense focus, and collaboration on all levels. Students acutely feel "the failure," and when they reach twenty, they'll likely erupt with cheers. Ask them why the overlapped words felt like "failure." Was it an honest attempt by someone to help the group achieve the goal? How can the group perceive these "failures" as true attempts by everyone to ensure the group's success?

When the group does succeed in reaching twenty, ask them why that moment felt so good. Common answers are "because we did it together," "because I realized I wasn't alone in this process," and "our success depended on all of us working together, not any one person."

*The Why*

To strengthen listening and focus, develop awareness, and build collaborative skills. This is a deceptively simple exercise that requires students to work collaboratively to achieve a common goal. It heightens awareness of collective energy in a room, and this in turn encourages connection between students and fosters team learning. Instead of focusing on the limitations of their surroundings, students realize the endless possibilities of collaborating with one another.

## CONCLUSION: TRANSITIONING TO THE ACTUAL LESSON

You've transformed the physical room into a shared exchange of offers between interested people, prepared your lesson in such a way as to shed the Us-vs.-Them template in both environment and attitude, and you've warmed up the students with exercises that ensure they're ready to connect, interact, and engage with whatever you have to offer.

How do you deliver?

Often, these exercises alone will do the trick. Students will welcome an opportunity to trust their impulses, move past some of their fears, and take joy in the connections that a united classroom will create. More often, you need to find a way to fill the lesson with the ideology the warm-ups have promised. You can't expect your students to remain excited about this shared stage space if you're not prepared to follow through.

One internet search will provide you with a thousand articles on pedagogy, the fall of the class lecture, and the need to break up lessons into twenty-minute intervals for fear of losing the attention span of the millennial generation. In chapter 2 we discussed your role as a performer in the classroom. Now that you're a performer who has created a space that inspires your students to leap over the dividing line and meet you on the shared stage, how can you continue to get them to engage? In the next chapter, we'll discuss what every performer needs to overcome those lines between your audience and you, and between your story and you: great acting partners—your students.

*Chapter Five*

# Your Students as Your Acting Partners

Whether it's your first day or your thousandth, you know you were hired for this job because of your strengths and skills, and your success depends on your collaboration with the perfect strangers you're about to meet. What if they're not very open with you? What if they aren't interested in collaborating? What if they don't like this material, or simply don't like *you*?

Is this a teacher facing their fears as they walk to their first day of class, or an actor en route to a first rehearsal?

Both.

Teachers and actors require the exact same ingredient: living, breathing partners that create a give-and-take relationship. We've explored ways to connect teachers more directly with their skills, the material, and environments of storytelling. Those processes bring us closer to our students. The next step is to inspire them to intentionally move from their "side" of the line to meet us in the middle. How?

By making the students our acting partners.

Though the act of teaching students might feel akin to the performer/audience relationship, that model is closer to Us vs. Them; with *us* being in the light, telling stories to *them*—those people—in the dark. The dividing line is not only psychological ("I'm telling this story and you are not") but also visual ("I'm onstage and you are not"). The model of actors working together better reflects the collaborative ideal that we're striving for.

Here's why: Though actors are keenly aware of audience energy and responses, they're trained for and must accept that audiences receive a story through the lens of their personal experiences. Actors can't crawl into the psyches of every single audience member to force them to like a play. It's a tough challenge when your job requires you to be under constant scrutiny and judgment from a roomful of perfect strangers.

Sound familiar?

Have you ever thought a student disliked you and then discovered they had a terrible experience with a previous teacher? Or encountered one who is resistant to discuss world affairs, and you later found they had a parent deployed to a danger zone? Like an actor, a teacher can't crawl inside the minds and psyches of their students and know the personal reasons they are struggling with the material, or with you.

Teachers are like actors in another way: an actor never gives up on their partner(s) onstage. Their commitment to collaboration and to the story compels them to stay in the ring and keep fighting, which is what teachers do every single day. We need to have faith we can reach every student.

Consider your students as active partners instead of simply "receivers" of the story. Like acting partners, when they feel the story can't be told without them, and that their "partner" (you) won't give up on them, their desire to bring themselves to the material—and you—increases.

A rehearsed play is eventually presented to an audience as a finished product. The story won't change: the lines are said in the same order by the same characters; the play is set. When you're teaching gravity, the story of gravity won't change; that apple is always going to fall in one direction—down. However, within that series of "set" aspects for a play, one thing remains flexible with the potential for spontaneity, and that's the dynamic between scene partners. The text won't change, and the character's objective won't change, but *how* the actors get there will be a little different each night.

Actors allow themselves to be influenced by everything surrounding them in each moment, and as long as they continue to collaborate together, they make the story come alive. Teachers can also allow themselves to be affected by what immediately surrounds them. Sure, gravity will always be gravity, but *how* gravity is understood can happen in new and dynamic ways, and it depends on your ability to engage and collaborate with your acting partner: your students.

That's why partnership is better. There's a reason the phrase "the show must go on" continues to ring true. The core of that cliché is rooted in the deep commitment actors have to their partners, and to the telling of the story. But the show can only go on if everyone commits to that principle so the responsibilities are shared. In this chapter we'll illustrate what tools teachers need to set the table for partnership. We'll then apply those concepts to exercises you can use to develop the acting-partner model of partnership and collaboration with your students.

**Rose**

The best onstage "save" I ever saw was when I was directing an off-Broadway production of *Pygmalion*, with Henry Higgins played by the wonderful Jay Nickerson. Because the theater was below street level, we sometimes had problems with mice and their larger cousins. So, the artistic director got a cat for the theater, which did the job nicely, and the stage manager's job each night was making sure the cat was locked in the office during shows. As you can imagine, the following was inevitable.

One night, the cat managed to get out of the office. During the scene where Henry Higgins is speaking to his mother (played by the unflappable Marlene May) in her parlor, seeking her approval while bemoaning the fact that Eliza isn't grateful, the cat decided to have a stroll right onto the stage. And I mean a leisurely amble; the cat was not daunted by the audience at all. Jay looked down and, without missing a beat, said, "Ah, there you are. Mother was looking for you earlier." And with one swift move, he scooped up the cat in his arm and began absentmindedly scratching it behind the ear as he tried to persuade his mother that he's actually the wounded party.

He treated the cat like an ally in battle, as if to say, "*Some*one thinks I'm important." It all happened so fast; the audience began laughing at both the "mistake" of the cat walking onstage and how "expected" Jay made it feel. To prove it takes a village, the quick-thinking actor who played the Maid, Melanie Hopkins, rushed onstage, made eye contact with Jay, and curtsied; Jay said, "Yes, I imagine it's her feeding time." He then handed the offending cat to Melanie (the cat, by the way, was rather limp and disinterested the whole time), and she took the cat offstage.

Not only did this "mistake" not stop Jay in his tracks, but he actually used it to bring new life to a scene that he and Marlene had been performing for a month and a half. The story was saved, and the theater cat had his debut, and retirement.

Can you imagine if Jay had stopped the scene, broken character, looked offstage, and yelled, "Will somebody please come and get this *%!#@! cat?" Nope. He stayed in character and took advantage of an opportunity, and all three actors worked together in that moment to support and feed the solution (and the cat).

## THINKING LIKE A PARTNER

In chapter 2, you completed "Personal Analysis," and that included a personal "check-in" so you're ready to work with your partners the moment you enter the room. Whether you achieve this with the physical and vocal prep or through analysis and self-reflections, try not to let your state of mind be the last thing on your list that you take care of. Flight attendants tell you to put on your own oxygen mask first before helping others; that's good life advice too.

## Shared Failure and Success

Reflect on your concept of failure and how that might connect to your own ego. As discussed in chapter 3, students need to fail at times in order to learn, and though failure needs to be acknowledged, it shouldn't be stigmatized. And *you* need to be able to fail too; otherwise, you'd never try anything new in your classroom. The more transparent you are with your students about the expectations of failure for you both, the stronger the foundation of trust will be for your partnership. Students will need to be reassured of what this means so there's no misunderstanding; you can't have them thinking that you intend to purposely fail at times in order to teach them something. Be clear that what you mean is, despite everyone's best efforts, they and you will both make mistakes.

If the idea of admitting to your students that you also make mistakes is too awful to contemplate, why is that? You know mistakes lead to discoveries—so why might you struggle to admit that that's true for you too? What could you gain by sharing that with your students? If you can joyfully embrace a mistake and celebrate it—"Ah! I made a mistake! That means I'm about to discover something new!"—what a fantastic example for your class. Christian De Matteo shares a great story:

> In my speech classes I teach them to acknowledge a moment of misspeaking and tell the story of a stuffy math teacher I had in high school who, attempting a biology analogy to explain a math concept, said the word "orgasm" instead of "organism." Rather than acknowledging, he desperately repeated "organism" with the ferocity of the words "Shut up!" to the class, who had fallen completely apart. Had he owned it, and made a follow-up joke about the mistake, the class would have been on his side, glad for the acknowledgment and even seeing him as an ally in keeping the class fun. Instead, he allowed himself to be the butt of the joke by showing his mortification, fueling the fire further.

Acknowledging you've made a mistake reinforces to your students that they aren't failures, even if their answers or efforts may be. It shows you'll support one another no matter what. Collaboration means never having to experience something alone.

## Principles of Collaboration: First Day Guidance from the Teacher

When you focus on building partnerships with your students, you create the bonds of ensemble (ensemble is any number of people collaborating and working toward a collective goal). When you meet for your first class, introduce expectations and ground rules that support collaborative relationships and build ensemble:

- A safe space. Assure them you'll do your best to create a safe and supportive environment and that you need their help to protect and nurture what you create together.
- The role of failure (a separate concept from grading). Failure is necessary for your class and for learning. Nurture the freedom for all to make mistakes, fail, and then try again. Acknowledge that grades are certainly going to be given, and they have the potential to achieve even stronger grades if they can let go of their initial fears of failure (more on that later). Tell them you need their permission to fail as well.
- Expectations of behavior. Have mutual respect for one another and for the work, have patience, and encourage and support one another. Clarity on structure and expectations encourages risk taking.
- Expectations of collaboration. Participation and completing assignments are important needs of the collaborative model; if Chris comes to class unprepared, or hasn't done the reading, he has robbed Julie of an idea that may have inspired her. If Arthur doesn't show up, he has robbed Chris of an insight that would have helped him understand the material better. Every action they take or don't take affects someone else. Urge everyone to ask, What does this class need from me today? How can I support the goal of all of us learning together?

## Collaborative Skills You Both Need to Build Partnerships

Connecting with another person is a process sometimes as mysterious as it is rewarding. We've all had moments when we've wondered, *Why isn't my friend/brother/spouse listening to me?* Actors encounter this daily, and their success depends on creating a strong give-and-take with partners. Like life, actors encounter partners who may be shy, reticent to open up, or self-involved. Let's face it: even when two people *want* to connect with one another, it can be hard.

Connection requires vulnerability, a willingness to listen and respond, and most of all, a level of empathy. That can be a risky human process. Ultimately, it's as simple as thinking "we" instead of "me," and then acting on that. As discussed earlier, the skills that actors use to create that "we" can be used in our classrooms: empathy, listening, observation, being present, awareness, spontaneity, flexibility, adaptability, stamina, risk taking, and honesty.

- Empathy: The ability to identify with, relate to, and be sensitive to the feelings of others. Eye contact is important to nurture this; however, with the ubiquitous use of smartphones, eye contact has become less common. It asks people to really see one another, which can be uncomfortable but is essential. Empathy in your classroom also means being sensitive to global and community events, and letting students talk when they need to.
- Listening and observation: Taking in what someone is saying and doing in a specific moment. Noticing tone, emotion, intention, and meaning. That is, we're not simply looking or hearing; we're *seeing* and allowing ourselves and our choices to be influenced by what we observe.

  - Can you tell by looking at a group of students who's prepared and who's not? Take a moment later to reflect on *why* you could tell, what each specific bit of body language expressed to you. Sometimes teachers—and actors—take in information so quickly that they chalk it up to being intuitive. And they are. But intuition is also rooted in specific observations we've made. If we can analyze and understand them more fully, we strengthen our ability to observe.
  - If your course content actually requires observation skills, introduce students to observation exercises. For example, *Observe 6* (see appendix G) requires two people to face each other, observe one another for a few seconds, and then turn their backs. One partner changes six things about their appearance (untie a shoe, remove a bracelet, and so on); then partners face each other again, and the other person must guess the six changes. Create a time limit for this; then have the partners switch. See appendix U for other simple observation activities.

- Being present: To be fully in the moment, focused, listening, and observing with full attention on the person you're engaged with and on the task that you're doing together. Not anticipating where the moment *will* go, not reflecting on what just happened—but to be fully present in a moment. When you obsess about a moment with a student that didn't go as well as you'd hoped, you're "in the past," and there's nothing you can do about it. Except to let that moment go.

  This frees you to be in the moment with each other, creating an opportunity for something new that *can* be better. You can get so focused on where you feel the moment *should* go that you're not present enough to see where it *could* go.
- Awareness: Being acutely conscious of what's around us and our observations and perceptions of those events and people. This includes awareness

of energy, being able to sense when a student's attention and focus drift or are misplaced.
- Spontaneity: Responding to impulses and stimuli in the moment. Spontaneity is rooted in inspiration, inspiration is connected to instinct, and instinct creates an impulse. If we're listening and responding truthfully in a moment, we won't need to stop and think about what to do next; we'll simply do it or say it.
- Flexibility and adaptability: Allowing yourself to be affected by your partner in the moment and responding spontaneously (without judgment) to choices and stimuli and adjusting to those new conditions.

  - For example, you may have prepared a lesson about the night Lincoln was assassinated. If students seem more interested in discussing John Wilkes Booth, approach the event through Booth's experience. Many won't know the reasons Booth shot Lincoln, or how he was able to succeed.

- Stamina: Sustained physical, vocal, and psychological effort. Some of you may be naturally gifted with strong stamina, but even if you are, that can change with age, schedules, and requirements. This is why we recommend extensive preparation work in chapter 2. If students see that your energy is flagging, they have less incentive to respond in kind.
- Risk taking: Willing to make choices out of your comfort zone. As teacher David Storck says, "It's not how far you go outside your comfort zone; it's how often."
- Honesty: Being truthful with yourself, your partner, and the material at hand. If you try to pretend everything's okay when it's not, the students will easily see through you. Admitting you're a little off will only increase your connection in the room. And students will feel more open to revealing a little about themselves.

Theater games can greatly help you and your students better connect to each of the above concepts. Refer to the appendices for examples and their benefits.

### Mike

I took a class on Chaucer in college taught by one of those great teachers. The professor would read *The Canterbury Tales* in Old English and then go back and explain them to us as if we were all on an adventure—full of excitement, joy, and energized engagement.

So it was obvious that something was wrong one morning: it was an 8:00 a.m. class, and for the first time the energy he brought to the room made it feel like 8:00 a.m. He stopped a few sentences into a reading, fanning both hands over his mouth, and his eyes grew glassy—not overly so though. This wasn't a breakdown. This was an honest moment of humanity from a person who was open to his class, his students, and everyone with whom he ever interacted.

He took a breath through his palms, lowered his hands, and said, "I'm sorry. I just found out my best friend died. Got the call in my office a few minutes ago." He paused, his eyes washing over us before returning to the middle distance, and none of us knew what to say.

After a moment, someone in the back spoke up: "It's okay, Professor." And another voice from the seats next to the windows: "Yeah, don't worry. We're sorry." And soon after, all our voices piped in, offering condolences and suggestions ranging from ending class for the morning so he could deal with it to all of us heading to the local diner for breakfast.

He laughed at that last one, breaking out of his moment of inner loss. He shook his head and said, "No, it's okay. Let's go on. I might be a little off today though." And he was a little off, but because of his honesty and our empathy, we met him more than halfway across the room, filling in the gap he couldn't. Not only did we have a great class, but also the next few courses I took with him held a special connection between all of us. He'd been honest in a way we didn't expect, and none of us ever forgot it.

## COLLABORATING WITH YOUR PARTNERS

It's one thing to know what collaborative skills are and what we *should* do with them, but how do we begin to actively apply them? In chapter 1, we outlined essential theater methods; through the lens of these five principles, your students will become your acting partners:

1. Yes And
2. Make Your Partner Look Good
3. Follow the Fear
4. Dare to Make the Obvious Choice
5. Take Care of and Support Your Partner

## Yes And

As discussed in chapter 1, Yes And is the heart and soul of acting; we commit to mutually supporting one another's choices and ideas. This is probably the most valuable principle for our classroom, and one of the easiest to achieve. There must be agreement between partners in order for a story to grow. In an improvisation, it could be the following:

"I have a confession: I love horror movies."

"That's great! I'm having a Halloween movie festival at my house. Wanna come?"

The offer of "horror movies" was accepted and was added to, building a story that could lead to a deepening friendship, a party that gets out of control, or two people deciding to make their own scary movie. But what if the exchange went another way?

"I have a confession: I love horror movies."

"Who the hell are you? Get lost."

The opposite of Yes And is No, But. In this example of No, But, the responder rejects the premise that they even *know* the other person. The story stopped dead in its tracks. How can we apply this in the classroom? We can take what our student/partner offers and build on it so they feel they are needed by the story and by their teacher. For example:

TEACHER: "What struck you most in last night's reading about sharks?"

LENA: "That they don't have bones . . ."

TEACHER: "Yes! And not having bones helps them—how?"

MICHAEL: "It helps them be more flexible, *and* that helps them to swim faster." (Michael has just said Yes And to the teacher's questions.)

CRISTINA: "Yes, and if it helps them swim faster, they can effectively catch more prey." (Cristina has just said Yes And to Michael's comment.)

KAILA: "Yes! And if they catch more prey, they're successful as a species and they'll survive."

Now, you could easily have said, "Good morning, class. As you know from last night's reading, sharks don't have bones, which has made them successful as a species for four hundred million years." It would save time, and you could get to the next point more quickly. What's the benefit of approaching this lesson via Yes And?

- Students feel needed by the teacher and their peers.

- Students experience positive collaboration in listening to one another and having their feedback accepted and added to. Their input and voices are valued.
- The story moves forward because everyone participates.
- There's collective ownership of the learning. Because it took four people to build the statement of fact about sharks, they all feel each contribution they made, and the lesson wouldn't be able to stand without each piece of information they offered.
- Bonus: They recognized doing the homework (reading assignment) freed them to confidently participate in a discussion (reinforcing the value of preparing for each class).

## Make Your Partner Look Good

For actors, this is about listening to and being generous with your partner. If you take care of your partner, you're taking care of the story. If you're not focused on *your* shining moment, you're better able to focus on the *story's* shining moment. If partners are working to make each other "look good," then they're listening, open and responsive, and applying Yes And, all for the benefit of the story. For example, in class discussion you ask,

"Who wants to share their thoughts about Charles Dickens?"

A student raises their hand and says, "I enjoyed *Great Explorations*."

You have two choices: you can say, "Wrong!" roll your eyes, correct them, and move on. Or you can make your partner look good. "You're in the ballpark, Monica. It's *Great Expectations*, but we can see how your mind might want to swap those words out. Dickens's novel does paint Pip as though he were an explorer trying to find his way through multiple worlds: graveyards, prison ships, and spooky houses—and the metaphor extends to how he navigates relationships. Someone define 'explorer' for us?"

VALERIAN: "They discover things."

TEACHER: "Yes! And what are some of the things Pip discovers?"

ASHLEY: "That you shouldn't assume things about people because of their looks or possessions."

TABITHA: "Yes! And that he shouldn't try to be something he isn't based on how he sees wealthy people live. He almost loses himself."

TEACHER: "Right! And what else does he discover about himself? Monica, you started us on this great journey; we need another guidepost from you."

Yes, the teacher kick-started this by asking about Dickens and corrected Monica—but it costs the teacher *nothing* to give ownership to Monica. In fact, it makes her partner look good, it inspires others to speak up (*Jeez, the teacher didn't make Monica feel bad for getting the book title wrong*), and encourages risk taking, and Monica ends up feeling supported and that her mistake turned into an opportunity—and everyone learned from it collectively.

Look, we get it: Monica may not have been thinking *at all* about Pip as an explorer of the human condition. But then again, maybe she *was*. Either way, again, it costs you nothing to give her the benefit of the doubt, help her save face while sharing the correct information and creating a terrific example of a mistake being a springboard for something useful and impactful.

*Pause in the List: A Few Words About Competition*

Much of our educational system is based on grades; someone is going to get an A, and someone will get a big, fat F. Grades inherently encourage competition to get that A, and that can ignite ego. In theater, we encourage actors to be competitive with only themselves, and if they collaborate, they get the A together. That is, they try not to measure their achievements and judge them as good or bad using their partner's accomplishments as the standard.

Students often drive themselves crazy wondering if their idea or choice is stronger, richer, or better than what their classmate just said. Or they may feel defeated because—though they worked their tail off—they got a B+ and their buddy sitting next to them got an A and barely put in any effort. Competition: Though it can have positive results, it can also feel unfair and can damage a student's confidence and desire to learn. To nurture partnership, try to lean less heavily on grades as a sole measurement of success. Encourage collaboration, and include their proficiency at teamwork as part of their grade consideration.

**Follow the Fear**

Renowned improv teacher Del Close said, "Follow the fear." What he meant was, try to do what scares you the most; your fear can be a divining rod to guide you to what may become your greatest strengths. One discovery actors make by following their fear is that it's the *fear* that's stopping them from growing and connecting with others, not "the thing" they're afraid *of*.

For example, an actor thinks, *I'm so afraid of being vulnerable*. If they listen to that fear, they'll be so afraid of *not* being vulnerable that they *won't* be. They're actually afraid they aren't *capable* of being vulnerable, and by giving in to the fear, it becomes a self-fulfilling prophecy. It's the fear itself, though, that keeps them from being vulnerable, not a lack of ability. Follow Close's philosophy in your classroom; acknowledge fear with your students, and because you've created a partnership with them, you'll follow the fear together.

Have an open discussion with students about the role of fear in learning. Most fears fall into the following categories: fear of failure, fear of rejection, fear of judgment, and fear of looking stupid. What do they think is the source of their fear? They don't need to share that with you or the class, but they need to know for themselves. If "fear" feels like too loaded a word for them, ask them to call it "the enoughs," for example, "I'm not smart enough," "I'm not original enough," and so on. What's the "enough" they're most afraid they lack?

Then ask them, "What's the worst thing that could happen?"

They may say, "I'll look stupid" or "I'll embarrass myself." Talk with them about the amount of energy they expend in worrying about "the worst." Obsessing about the fear magnifies its power, and imaginations keep feeding that fear.

If they let themselves experience their worst-case scenario, they experience the reality of it. True, nobody actually *likes* facing their fear, so what incentive could help them try to follow it?

You—and their partners—will be there to catch them.

You can make mutual support a fun requirement for the class; Patricia Ryan Madson, author of *Improv Wisdom*, taught a class wherein if a student made a mistake or misspoke, they had to take a bow, and everyone was required to applaud. Silly? Sure, but after a few times the stakes of being "wrong" were reduced, and students took greater risks in her class. So, when they struggle with following their fear, demonstrate they aren't alone. Examples:

- If you're teaching a writing class, ask the students to write a short play in which they and their fear appear as characters. What do they say? If they add characters and cast a classmate in this play, they'll also see that the fear affects everyone. Have the students read aloud what they've written and embody the characteristics of the fear. Students sometimes discover that their fear has admirable qualities (persistence, strength, confidence)—qualities they themselves may wish they had more of.
- If it's a science class, ask, what if Alexander Fleming returned from his vacation in 1928, and finding mold on his petri dishes, quickly threw them away because of his fear of being accused of having a sloppy lab? How would things be different today without penicillin? They'll have fun imagining the many ways things could go terribly wrong. Ask them to write a dialogue between Fleming and his fear, and have one student play Fleming, and another his fear. Prompt them to respond to fear's actions toward Fleming, knowing what they now know about the magnitude of his discovery.

By identifying creative ways to explore their fears together, you'll nurture mutual support and create a shared road map, making following their fear an uplifting adventure.

## Dare to Make the Obvious Choice

This is an important follow-up to "Follow the Fear." In his book *Impro*, Johnstone writes that actors often worry about being "original." This concept ties directly into the idea of competition. "What can I talk about that nobody else will think of? Was Professor Floyd more impressed with my answer than anyone else's?" None of this has anything to do with true original thought; these ideas connect to the worry, "How am I measuring up *against* that *other* person?"

When Johnstone nurtured originality and risk taking in his students, he encouraged them to dare to make the obvious choice." He didn't mean "obvious" as in "dull"; he meant to make a choice that is obvious to *you*; what is obvious to *you* will *not* be obvious to anyone else. To want to be like, or better than, someone robs you of your originality. If a student commits to their first idea, their originality is doing the talking. If they judge the worth or popularity of the idea, they're no longer daring to make the obvious choice.

You can encourage your students to make their obvious choice in several ways:

- Do lightning-round exercises; have them do or say something quickly. This helps them to know what their impulsive—and obvious—answers and choices are. It doesn't give them time to judge or throw away an idea. Ask, "Give me one-word adjectives to describe Pip's character traits—go!"
- Have them do free-writes in the class. Give a set time (five or ten minutes), a prompt to respond to, and instructions that their pen or pencil can't leave the page. If they get stuck, tell them to keep repeating the previous word or phrase they've written until something else comes to them. They could even keep writing, "I'm stuck. Why? I have nothing else to say. I wish I did but . . ." and riff on that until something else comes to them. This helps them connect to their obvious choices, brainstorming about what that could lead to, all without being able to judge, edit, or erase.
- Another writing exercise that adds collaboration is Steve Ansell's Pass the Story. Each student starts their own fictional short story by writing the first sentence. The teacher times it and announces, "Pass the Story." Every student must pass the story to the next, read the first sentence, and add the second sentence to it. The exercise proceeds until the original writer gets their story back. Encourage students to try to unify the story by sticking to the plot handed to them. If it's a story about a guy walking down the street

to buy milk, let that be the story. Don't be tempted to try to add zombies or superheroes.

Now, what about *you*? How free do you feel to dare to make your obvious choices? Do you worry how students will perceive you if you work from your obvious—and therefore, most personal—choices? If your students are supporting one another, trust that they'll also support *you* if you commit to your obvious choice, especially if your choice may not lead things where you wanted them to go.

You may fear getting off track in class, and that could happen. But think of the power of taking a risk and making a mistake in front of students. What a great learning lesson for them if they see you give yourself permission to try, risk, and fail, and you acknowledge that to them. You'll inspire them and make it safer for them to do that as well.

For example, you've been assigned a class that's been on the books for years, and the syllabus you inherited has a reading list that hasn't been changed in a decade. You know several new and dynamic books on the subject, but you don't want to make waves so you leave the reading list as is. Fast-forward to the day the first reading assignment is due. You ask, "Who would like to start off today's discussion about the reading?" Deafening silence. You observe glances exchanged between students and some fidgeting.

You prompt again, and someone says, "I fell asleep reading it." A wiseacre pipes up and says, "It might help if we weren't reading the fifth edition of a book written in 1973." The rest of the students heave a sigh of relief and chime in: "Omigod, it was so *boring*"; "The author uses 'he/him/the man' the whole time; does he know women were invented before 1973?"; and so forth.

Now, you have two choices: You can say, "I make the assignments around here. You'll read it and learn." Or you can be honest: "I think I was a little afraid of taking a risk in changing the old syllabus. If I expect you to take risks in your learning, I should take more risks in my teaching. Let's discuss this reading in terms of its problems as well as any still relevant insights. Don't be afraid to be harsh."

## Take Care of and Support Your Partner

A variation of another improv rule is never leave anyone behind, even if it means saving yourself. In acting, we take care of our partner by saying Yes And, and by lifting them up when they're struggling. Empathy and listening play a big role; if your partner is having a bad day, you have two choices: support the partner, or save yourself. If a partner blanks on a line, the other person could stop, turn to the audience, and say, "It's *her* turn to talk, not mine!" Or they could offer the partner a supportive choice to help them with whatever may be blocking them.

For example, the actor playing Tessie is supposed to say the line "You apologize to me right now, Delmont Williams!" But instead, she's staring blankly, and silently, with terror at the actor playing Delmont. He can add a line that will help trigger her memory. "Tessie, I know you're mad at me . . . but nothing you could say or do is going to make me apologize." Actors understand that if they abandon their partner, they abandon the story.

What happens if a teacher only takes care of the students who have all the answers, or who seem to especially love the subject? We've also all had That Student who aces every question, and is your go-to person when no one raises their hand after a prompt. "Please share your thoughts about last night's reading on Neolithic migration patterns in Western Europe. Anyone? Yes, Lisa. Thank you. Now what did those patterns mean for the development of agriculture in the British Isles? Anyone? Yes, Lisa . . ."

No matter how tempting, we need to move beyond the "Lisas" in our classes; otherwise, the others won't feel essential to the story. If you support every student, especially those who are struggling, you teach that everyone is needed, and everyone is responsible for one another.

### Mike and Rose

Our colleague David Storck, who is simply one of the best improvisation teachers on the planet, shares his favorite story about dedication in an ensemble in *Ensemble Theatre Making: A Practical Guide.*

> One of the most memorable improv shows I've ever seen was absolutely terrible. Try as they might, nothing the group did that night seemed to work. The scenes went from bad to worse. The audience grew more uncomfortable as the minutes passed. The final scene of the show turned out to be on a ship. As you might expect, before long someone shouted "we're sinking!" It was an effort to inject some energy, stakes, and excitement into the scene. But alas, the scene continued to struggle. As the players began to lower themselves to the floor to indicate the sinking of the ship, they were all desperately trying to get in a funny one-liner that might offer some small measure of redemption. The lights slowly began to fade. At that moment, three members of the group who were not in the scene, but standing nearby, jumped onto the sinking ship. They all went down with the ship. They were committed to each other, no matter the circumstances, even through this great adversity.

> Those three performers could have remained to the side, away from the mess on stage, but they chose to jump in with their mates, knowing they could do nothing to help other than to show "we're with you."

There will be days when a student is emitting a "whatever you do, please, by Grabthar's Hammer, don't call on me" vibe. Focus on that student who wants to be avoided; if you don't, you won't help them with whatever they're struggling with. Try calling on them first so they don't spend the entire class biting their nails and obsessing about when or if you'll call on them.

If the class seems exhausted, you can be generous and say, "Everyone looks a little tired today; Ahsan, can you help start us off with a recap of last night's reading assignment?" In this way, you're asking Ahsan not for new ideas but to help you and the class, and to simply state what the assignment was. It may even inspire Ahsan to contribute as the class goes on.

For an exercise that demonstrates taking care of one another, try *Dinner Party* outlined in appendix C. It's simple, it's physical, and it brings home the lesson of all for one, and one for all in a fun and challenging way.

## THE ROLE OF STATUS IN PLAYING WITH YOUR PARTNERS

Some suggestions in this chapter may have ignited concerns that if you treat your students as your acting partner, you'll lose your status in the classroom. You won't permanently lower your status to your students and abdicate your position of responsibility, but if you learn to become an expert status player, you'll be able to achieve your goals by playing both high *and* low status.

In chapter 2 we discussed status as the hierarchical differences between, or exchange of, power in a relationship. In exploring status, examine what your personal preferred status is. Of course, our status shifts all the time, but given your druthers, are you more comfortable leading with high status ("Don't come near me; I bite") or low status ("Don't bite me; I'm not worth the trouble")? Neither is good or bad; it's simply information about yourself.

Your preferred status may also depend on whom you're with in each moment. If you're with a parent, whether you're twenty-five or forty-five, you may defer to lower status—taking up a little less space, lowering your eyes, and so forth. If you're with an old friend, your default may be a higher status—making eye contact, leaning forward, and taking up more space. The key idea here is status is fluid, and is dependent upon your relationship to someone or something else.

Can a person play lower status and get what they want? Absolutely. Think of the character Verbal Kint in *The Usual Suspects* (spoiler alert): he plays supreme low status. He's twitchy and physically clumsy (low status to his body), falls out of a chair he sits in (low status to the chair), prattles on without a break (low status to his own voice), and shrinks away from people (low status to the people and to the space; he yields territory). However, later in the film we find out he is actually the master criminal Keyser Soze, whose status is so high others fear to say his name out loud.

In the final scene, we watch the character physically transform from low to high status in his walk, his posture, and his attitude toward the objects and people surrounding him. He goes from yielding to space to taking up *more* space (increasing his height); moving with grace (high status to his body), he's not in a rush (high status to time—and to the police behind him), and he glides into the passenger seat of his chauffeur-driven car (high status to the car and to the chauffer).

Now, can a person aim for high status and *not* get what they want? Sure. Think of the person ahead of you at the DMV, yelling at the clerk. The more indignant and loud they become, the more power they seem to *lose* in relation to the quiet and calm DMV clerk. The clerk has all the power, and they know it. They don't *need* to "assert" themselves; they *are* powerful, and they're confident in their authority. This drives the person trying to raise their status even crazier.

A person can certainly *try* to raise their status, but if their partner doesn't yield, or deflects the attempt, their attempt will fail and their status will actually *drop* instead. If someone is very pointedly trying to raise their status, they can appear insecure, lowering status further. Rose often cautions her acting students to be wary of any director who feels the need to say, "I'm the director." Everyone knows that; so why would a director seek respect by announcing their title, instead of seeking respect through the competency of doing their job? If you're thinking about a time when you may have said, "I'm the teacher. You need to do the homework when I say so" and it had no effect—that's why!

There are a number of tactics that Johnstone describes as useful in the classroom. A simple one is using eye contact. If a student asks you a question, try looking them directly in the eye as you respond, and then look away. But what if you found yourself immediately glancing back after breaking eye contact? The first example is high status: confident, direct, and clear, and *you* decided when the exchange was over. The second example implies insecurity as if you're "checking in" to see how the student responded to you.

Remember that words, volume, or gestures alone don't guarantee a particular status. It's what you choose to specifically do with those choices that make the status high or low. Johnstone also recommends you try raising or lowering status incrementally, just a little at a time, and gauge the impact. This will also help you gain greater awareness of how much power you do or don't need to exert in a moment.

Let's go back to the earlier example of Ahsan, the "By Grabthar's Hammer, please don't call on me" student. Is he playing high status or low status? If low status (eyes lowered, arms crossed across his chest), could you lower your status to help him participate?

"Ahsan, you bailed me out of a jam last week when you reminded us that there actually *are* primary-source images of life from thirty-five thousand years ago, in the form of the many paintings in the Chauvet-Pont d'Arc Cave in France. I'd said something glib about there being no cameras to help us know for sure what life in ancient times looked like. I shouldn't have said that. Thank you for reminding us that we did have ancient artists expressing daily life on those cave walls."

You've lowered your status by raising Ahsan's; you've expressed gratitude to him for correcting you and assured him that he added something valuable to the class. "Can I lean on you again to help us get started today?" You've lowered your status further by expressing need, and you raise his status further because you specifically need *his* help at this moment.

Now, if Ahsan digs in and says, "I can't, not today," you can either give him a pass, saying, "I'm sure someone else is eager to jump in," or you could say, "Well, let's start with what you gave us last week. Who went home and looked up those amazing cave paintings?" You raise the status of other students by assuming their interest and desire to contribute, and raise Ahsan's status by reassuring him that others will support him in whatever he's going through.

You also know Ahsan obviously has an interest in those cave paintings; by focusing on something of personal interest to him, you increase the chances he'll want to participate. You also raise your own status—not at Ahsan's expense but in your guidance of the discussion. That is, you're so confident that you're fine with lowering your status if it helps a student participate.

Could you approach Ahsan using high status? Sure—it simply depends on what you think will work best. Higher status doesn't mean you'll turn into Severus Snape (or Albus Dumbledore, for that matter). And low status doesn't mean you're weak or indecisive (like Gollum). If you opt for higher status, use humor whenever possible. It's one of the strongest arrows in your quiver, and it helps to take away any "sting" a student could associate with having their status "lowered" in the hierarchy.

Yes, higher status might mean, "Come on. You *know* that participation in class discussions is 20 percent of your grade." You may have raised your status but at the expense of dragging out the ghost of grades and that there's retribution for silence (see Professor Snape above). However, if you take on a game show persona—"Come on, Ahsan, guess correctly, and you may have a trip to Acapulco behind Curtain Number 3!"—he still may not have anything to offer, or zero understanding of the reference, but he'll be laughing, more relaxed, and more open to you and the process through the fun you've just offered in the status exchange.

## FINAL WORD: SACRIFICE

To be a partner with your students involves a measure of sacrificing a traditional idea about being "the Teacher." It can appear as if you're relinquishing authority; by playing lower status, you might feel as if you're weaker than the student, or by treating them as a partner you might think they're enjoying an "unearned" place in the hierarchy. This can be tough on your ego; however, remember that as a teacher, you're an outstanding chess player.

You became a teacher for a reason, and you're good at this. You always know where the game is headed, at least four to five moves in advance, and that in the end you'll still be the teacher in charge. By sacrificing *your* shining moment (the one who knows the material inside and out), you place the focus on the *goal's* shining moment: the student's collaborative learning—not only what they learn but also *how* they learn. Like actors working together, this approach will take time and exploration, and will require sacrifice and commitment. The collective investment that you and your students will enjoy in learning will be worth it, always.

*Chapter Six*

# The Educator as Director

Though we've developed a collaborative, creative partnership with our students, we still carry the weight of the higher status in that partnership. We must. Leadership is essential to any group endeavor. However, how often we call attention to our authority and leadership is a different matter, and the role of the theater director is a perfect model to preserve this collaboration. A theater director, like an educator, is a member of the ensemble *and* the leader of it. It's our job to bring together various collaborators and guide them in uniting their unique contributions so the world of the play might be realized.

Sometimes, a director gets to wear both hats: that of a partner in the telling of a theatrical story and that of a leader, guiding the story through the creative process. Directors use some of the techniques discussed in chapter 5, while adding concepts discussed throughout this chapter. Like the director, a teacher can lead the ensemble while at the same time balance the characteristics of acting partner.

Inevitably, questions arise in the acting partner scenario about leadership and the place of authority in a relationship built on mutual trust. How do you bridge that divide, maintain the objectivity of a partner, and still earn their trust as a leader? And how do you avoid the pitfalls of appearing as another parent, a rule enforcer, and an authority figure against which to rebel?

In short, students might be your acting partner, but you're still their teacher. Though directors don't give actors grades, we do walk the tightrope of a collaborative relationship in which we are the higher-status partner because we have the added responsibility of being *in charge*. Directing techniques only strengthen the ability to remain open to a collaboration while being a dynamic ensemble leader.

## HOW TO USE THEATER DIRECTING IN THE CLASSROOM

Many audience members have no idea what a director did to the play they just watched. For the entire two-hour production, they will laugh and cry and applaud, and they'll say to the director, "Good job. You told them where to stand and where to walk well. Oh, and the costumes were beautiful. Where'd you get them?" Similarly, people will sometimes say to a teacher, "You're so lucky you get summers off! What do you do with all that spare time?" Few understand what our jobs actually *are*.

Yet your former students have learned from you, gained proficiency in a subject and its field, and launched careers. They navigate relationships and conversations and, in general, are good citizens who contribute to society. How often do they get stopped and told, "Wow, you must have had a great teacher"?

Directors and teachers coach, encourage, teach, critique, and assess. A theater director creates an environment in which all collaborators trust one another and use their discoveries to create the story they've all gathered to tell. They create this environment through applying a well-practiced structure to the rehearsal process, a structure akin to that of a good party, with the director as its host.

### The Host of the Party

In *Ensemble Theatre Making*, the authors point out that educators make great accomplishments by applying a similar party-host philosophy.

> Once the party has begun, your job is to fuel the guests; provide good food, keep their drinks fresh, and let them do what they do best; be themselves. Don't micro-manage or steer conversations to force your agenda. Stay attentive to needs and be open to pleasant surprises. If someone gets drunk or obnoxious, put them in a cab. If there's a spill, clean it up. What we're talking about here, without using the actual term, is creating a strong ensemble. (Bonczek and Storck 2012, 1)

A good party needs good leadership. You can't throw a party, invite everyone you like, and then sit around, waiting for them to show up and hope they'll bring a good mood and fun stories. You create the physical space, identify the purpose of the party, set the mood, and show them what this journey will entail.

That's exactly what you can do in your classroom.

1. On the first day, welcome them to the party and introduce yourself as the host. "Good morning. I'm Professor X, and I'll be your host in Genetic Evolution 101." Watch their body language when you apply

this metaphor, and observe how that body language evolves as you tell them a bit about yourself—who you are and why you're throwing this party—instead of falling into the repetitive rote rhetoric of "I'm your teacher and now let's look at the syllabus." Your students will begin to smile, lean in, and engage.
2. Tell them why you're so excited about this class and all the discoveries you hope to make together. What elements of your life, personally and professionally, make you excited to be there? Show them you're as exuberant about the subject as you hope they'll become. Let them in as much as you're comfortable doing, and then . . .
3. *Pass the ball.* You know who *you* are, and you know why you're here; they don't. Share the space. When you're playing a game, how does it make other players feel when one person holds onto the ball too long? Imagine this feeling in your students, ready to take their turn, and to take the ball and pass it. Share the space, and pass the ball.
4. Ask *them* to introduce themselves and share what they hope to get out of this class. Give them time and space to reveal, as you have done, where they are in their lives and what brings them to your classroom—even if the answer is, "I'm required to take this class." Let the line be a fun, honest quip at the introductory stage of your party. Encourage them to pass the ball if they're hugging it a bit too long. What makes them *want* to pass it on? Knowing they're needed by others and that everyone needs the ball that is now in their hands.
5. Tell them what kind of party this is, and be specific. Be clear in the policies and procedures of your classroom, while at the same time maintain the metaphor in which you're the host. Teachers and party hosts need to hold a measure of authority while they create a collaborative environment. A theater director describes the policies and rules for the production of the play during the first rehearsal.Make sure your own policies (and those of the institution) are clear. This way, the students will know what kind of party this is, and what the expectations are. Telling them it's a party doesn't *make* it a party; knowing what they're expected to bring, and then watching them "bring it," makes a fun gathering.

## Responsibilities of the Host (the Director and Teacher)

To create the environment and inspire risk taking, directors first encourage ideas without judgment. An actor starts a scene by making a choice that doesn't work for us? It's okay. Another actor's ideas go completely against our concept for the play? Let it happen. At least for a while. Eventually, we can address all those issues with our partners and correct them—only after they've had a chance to try their choice to see if it works. We let our students take risks, try, fail, and learn from the process.

Immediately stopping a student's attempt and telling them they're wrong—the No, But response—is generally the wrong one. It cuts off the creative impulse and puts walls in the way of your collaborative endeavor that might never come down. At the same time, that No, But response might be our *first* impulse; we're tired, we're annoyed with a particular student, or maybe our favorite baseball team lost a big one the night before in the twelfth inning.

Sometimes, when we shouldn't, we tell the student no and then dismiss them a little further with *but*: "No, you can't hand it in late. But you can go back to your desk." Instead, to provide encouragement we try to respond with Yes And, avoid negativity, offer them something positive, *and* add something engaging and creative. "Yes, I noticed you didn't hand in the assignment on time. And I'd like to meet with you to discuss why." Every good party host, after all, knows to use Yes And: "Yes, we're out of chips. And I've got ten more bags in the cabinet."

## When Someone Puts a Lampshade on at the Party: Challenges in the Classroom

Directors and teachers share a powerful level of commitment to their classes and projects. Teachers can't give up on a student or a classroom any more than a director can shrug off a play halfway through the rehearsal process. We're committed to our students, our lessons, and our creative approach to delivering the material. Directors use strategies in rehearsals to untangle problems and find solutions that unite the ensemble's efforts behind the goal.

*Party Challenge 1: Someone's Being a Drag*

What do you do when students aren't participating, or fulfilling their end of the bargain?

What characteristics do you notice in the group? Sometimes throwing a party means inviting your closest friends and you all immediately slide into your old routines and stories. Sometimes though, you need to plan a few games to get people warmed up to one another. The following are some brief examples, or scenarios, to follow during class sessions.

- Scenario: Midterm stress or other anxiety

  - Strategy: Try a game of *Three-Headed Alien* (see appendix J) to brighten the mood and relax the room. This game is fun and inevitably gets students laughing and also encourages listening, risk, and connection.

- Scenario: Bickering and snapping; grated nerves from spending too much time together

  - Strategy: Have them do a round of *Walk and Rename Objects* (See appendix K). This will get them physically active, energize their focus and commitment, and give them a fun and imaginative way to reclaim their world around them. As a bonus, it will help them notice more opportunities surrounding them.

- Scenario: Exhausted students with sleepy eyelids, slouched so low in chairs that they're about to fall to the floor

  - Strategy: Time for something physical; try *What Are You Doing?*, *Dinner Party*, or *Freeze Tag* (see appendices L, C, and E).
  - Strategy: If there's room, get them in a circle for a round of *Zing* (see appendix M), or play a game of *Slow-Motion Tag*: it's like traditional Tag, but they can't move quickly, and as soon as "It" catches someone, they have to freeze in place until everyone is "caught." It's silly, simple, fun, and won't take up much time.

- Scenario: Distracted students who don't pay attention to anything you say or do

  - Solution: A good eye-contact game is always helpful. It encourages concentration and focus and practices empathy, which has been sorely affected by excessive screen time in this generation of students.
  - Strategy: A great exercise for this is "Stop/Go." Have your students walk around the room. The objective is to not touch anything in the room or each other with any parts of their bodies. You announce "Go!" and "Stop" when you think it's appropriate. Then add a new wrinkle: they must make eye contact with different people throughout the next walk around the room, still not making physical contact with anyone or anything. This time, when you say "Stop," everyone in the room must be making eye contact with someone else. If they don't have someone, they must look around until they find a pair of eyes. They may initially be uncomfortable with the eye contact, but that very aspect, and the empathy it develops, nurtures so much else that will help them, in and out of the classroom. After a few attempts at Stop/Go, check in and ask the students what they've noticed about how it affects them. Over time, they can share what they notice about changes in their learning. If the students recognize the reasons they were asked to do the game, and experience the results, they can request it from the teacher when they feel their own need of it.

- Scenario: Three weeks from spring break and the students are already out the door

  - Strategy: Go outside! Take them out to a lawn or empty lot, and give them some exercises. With all this extra room, beautiful weather, and suddenly excited students, you can try something new. Play a game of *Explosion Tag* (see appendix D) and then go back to the lesson plan.

*What Doesn't Work*

No good party host can just walk away and slam the door: the No, But response. You can't greet that group of tired, unresponsive students with annoyance and disregard. "If you won't participate, here's an assignment you can do while I grade papers." Not only does this break trust, freeze the warmth you've brought to the room, and slow the learning process for those who didn't do the assignment, but also it undercuts *your* confidence. There's always something you can do to turn the party around.

When you have students who are lacking in concentration, spend a few minutes energizing and encouraging them. This will bring focus, listening, and connection to the lesson.

*Party Challenge 2: "Was I Supposed to Bring the Chips?" The Unprepared Student; or, "The Dog Ate My Ambition"*

In rehearsals, directors sometimes face an unprepared actor. He shows up and hasn't memorized his lines or doesn't remember where to be on the stage and is wandering into the wrong areas of the set. Or into someone else. In these cases, we can correct it: "You need to memorize your lines by tomorrow. Don't trip over Bob and fall on the floor again." However, that doesn't account for the other actors in the scene who *are* prepared.

Presumably you have a large number of students who have shown up with the work done, are ready to discuss, and are even excited to continue work on a project. The unprepared student, like the unprepared actor, can threaten the trust you've all created together. Directors determine how to point out these failures without hampering the actor's process, without compromising the concept that failure is necessary and essential for discovery, and without embarrassing them.

Likewise, you need to address the unprepared student while respecting those who've met their responsibilities. This also keeps the learning process moving forward so everyone is where they need to be in the overall process—together.

For example, you've given a homework assignment:

- A psychology class group project: Every group gets one of Maslow's Hierarchy of Needs (five categories of human needs divided into physiological, safety, love/belonging, esteem, and self-actualization) and, after a class discussion, writes and performs a scene depicting it.
- A biology class individual assignment: Each student reads the chapter on skin diseases and must perform a short scene in the classroom as a sick patient, describing the symptoms of one of the covered skin diseases until the entire class, playing the "doctor," can diagnose.

The day the assignment is due arrives, and several students stare at you as if they're in the wrong class. "I didn't know we were supposed to actually *write down* the scene about Maslow's stuff," or "I thought we were only supposed to *skim* the chapter."

*Solutions that Work*

Solution 1: Acknowledge the failure to complete the assignment without shaming the students and encourage accountability, integrity, and the partnership essential to collaborative learning. Someone who didn't do the homework might still be able to participate in a class discussion. Call on them, and bring them into the conversation. Don't let them rely on "I didn't do the reading so I can't help."

Strategy: "Mr. Thomasson," you say. "You didn't do the reading so you don't know what Maslow thinks are our most important needs. What's most important to you? Love? Self-esteem? Tell me in your own words. One of the biggest, most important needs you have." Maybe he'll buy in and say, "Love. Love of self. Love of others. Love of dogs and cats." Or maybe he'll still shrug and say, "Pizza." But you can use that! Turn to the next student who *did* do the reading. "That's great! Ms. Obregon, how do you think Maslow would rate pizza?"

You've continued a class discussion while including those who didn't do the reading. You kept it positive and entertaining, which makes students *want* to participate more and increases the likelihood the students will do the reading next time.

Solution 2: Encourage unprepared students through alternative or additional work. Make it clear that if they didn't do the reading or homework, they need to step up in a different way and listen and learn. Include an unprepared student in a group with prepared ones. Give the unprepared student a different task than the rest of the group. He will need to rely on an ability to improvise, to stay connected, and to offer ideas in order to receive *any* grade on the assignment.

Strategy: If the unprepared student is in the "self-esteem" group of the Hierarchy of Needs, she can contribute to the script, even without knowing the specific definitions. The group decides to write the script about a student who doesn't do her homework and is put in a group and expected to be a reliable member. She must provide examples of how this inclusion helps her self-esteem and how having understanding from others instead of judgment helps her be more responsible in the future.

Strategy: For the skin disease example, the group can create the scenarios and the unprepared student must perform them in front of the room. Although George didn't do the reading, with the collaborative help of the students in his group, he learns how to perform the physical characteristics of someone with chicken pox, and he also retains that knowledge for upcoming tests.

Strategy: There's always a good old-fashioned office meeting, in which you guide the unprepared students toward a realization. This reaffirms the connection and trust you've brought to the party. You're going to hold them accountable going forward, raising the stakes of what happens if they don't do the work. "I'll get an F *and* the professor will be disappointed *and* I'll have to go to her office."

Most important, you're there to offer additional help and support if there's a legitimate reason they didn't do the homework (they don't want to admit they can't afford to buy the book, or they have a learning disability they're embarrassed about).

*What Doesn't Work*

If you announce to the student, "Hey, you didn't do the homework . . . guess you fail this assignment," the following occurs:

- Dread: Every student, no matter who they are, has always dreaded that sentence.
- This kills the room. If only half of your students did what they were supposed to do, you can go forward with that half and complete the activity for the day. But the other half is still in the room and you haven't found a way to strengthen the ensemble through failure.
- Sure, they deserve the F. If you give them the grade and don't address the issue beyond that, they might still be unprepared tomorrow. They could continue to be distracting today. They'll feel resentful and left out and bring that energy back the next time. You've broken the trust brought to the room and affected the process of learning—yes, even though it's their fault.

Even facing unprepared students provides a great opportunity to build trust, from those who didn't prepare as well as those who did. Encouragement reassures the class that you'll protect the learning environment for *everyone* and will inspire your students to hold themselves more accountable. It might not solve the plethora of problems that caused the student to be unprepared in the first place, but it keeps your ensemble together, keeps the story moving forward, and the important lessons continue to be instilled.

*Party Challenge 3: The Uninvited Guest—That Memo from the Administration (State Testing, Classroom Visits, Room Changes, Fire Drills, Holidays)*

Directors are experts at adapting rehearsal plans to stay on schedule for the hard deadline of an opening night. We've worked at various rehearsal studios and theaters that have been hit with fire drills, leaky roofs, vermin infestation, and yes, cats who are supposed to be catching rats but decide to stroll onstage during a performance instead. Yet, everyone in that room is looking *to us* for a recovery plan.

Teachers face these issues all the time. You've got your lessons planned, and the students are engaged and ready. Then the administration strikes. The students need to take a placement test. Or you have to cancel class to go to a teacher training. A sudden policy-change email greets you moments before you walk into the classroom. Fire drills. The horrifying and necessary active shooter drills. *Something* is going to happen during the semester, and you'll have less time, energy, and preparedness than you expected.

Solution: Admit that we, directors and teachers, are just as lost as our actors and students. We need to dispel the myth that leadership means the leader is always stalwart and steady. We're allowed to take a moment to figure things out for ourselves and our ensemble, and to guide all of us back on course. When we're clear that we don't see ourselves as perfect, that we're learning too, students will relate and connect to us as fellow *humans*.

- Strategies:

  - Be up front about it: "This was an unexpected disruption, but let's breathe, regroup, and see what we can find now that we're back." Some great discoveries can come out of such "we're all in this together" regrouping. And students will often have a better idea than we do about how to meet the challenge.
  - As always, regroup through theater games: Try a quick round of *Zing* (appendix M), *Come Join Me* (appendix B), or *What Are You Doing?* (appendix L). Have fun and encourage risk taking within the games. This will help them make new discoveries that you may be able to tie back into the material. You'll make more progress in spending twenty minutes here than if you try to force them back on schedule via a rushed lesson.

- Ask the students to get into their groups outside of class and come back prepared with a presentation: Technology lets students easily find time to meet and have an open dialogue about their work. To prevent them from balking at the idea of *more* homework, make it clear that this assignment would be "instead of" the lost lesson and that it's to give *them* their money's worth. They've paid their tuition, and you don't want unforeseen circumstances to cheat them out of what they're owed.
- Bring it to them as a question: "You and I got delayed by the administration. I need your help to solve the problem. How could you all make up the lost lesson—without an onerous amount of time added to your homework/personal time? Creative suggestions? Extra credit?" Guide the students to your idea if you have one, but involve them in the decision-making process, giving them ownership over the assignment and the extra work they're about to do.
- Conspiratorial Bonus Motivation: When the administration is the cause of unexpected (and potentially unwanted) change in the classroom, you have a great opportunity to bond students, and bond *with* them, even further. Create a common obstacle in the administration's sudden state-mandated test or new attendance-taking requirement."I know we've got a lot to do, but I got this email from the administration today. Let me read it to you, and let's see if we can find a solution together." This reinforces your part in the ensemble and gives students agency in facing this new and unexpected requirement.
- Try a different assessment strategy instead of a test: A game of *Jeopardy!* (you do, after all, have the questions written out already). Create teams randomly, picking names out of a hat (don't let *them* pick, or everyone will try to grab Lisa because she knows everything about mathematical theory or Tom because he picks his teeth on axioms).
- Play a game of *Three-Headed Alien* (appendix J): Guide the students in working together to answer the questions.
- Give an oral quiz as a game, exercising your skills of observation and awareness: Which students seem confident in the material? Whose eyes are darting from side to side, looking for a life preserver from a friend? You have time-tested observation skills to help students in need, and now you're given a roomful of visual cues that you can act on!
- Have the students work together to design their own game: They will quiz one another in all aspects of the course curriculum you need them to know. They can work in groups, ad-lib ideas in a class discussion, or in a computer room, create something more complex. They'll have fun and study for the test at the same time.

**Rose**

Theater History used to be the one course in our curriculum every student dreaded. Thousands of years of facts, dates, memorization, and reading old and bad translations of old and (mostly) good plays; it was a rare student who enjoyed that class. Then we hired a new teacher, Amy Hughes. Amy had a lot of new ideas she wanted to try for Theater History, and we said "Absolutely! Have at it!" and silently I thought, *and good luck with that.*

A few weeks into the semester, I was walking to my office and was nearly run down by two of my breathless BFA acting students, Collin and Ugo. They had stacks of papers and were wearing odd hats; one had on some sort of ascot tie thing, and they were both laughing and jostling one another as they ran toward the stairwell. I yelled. "Whoa there! Where's the fire? An audition?"

They grinned ear to ear, and Collin said "No! We're debating neo-classicism in Theater History today, and we get to present!" Ugo said, "We were just preparing, and we lost track of time—we're gonna be late!" I said, "Then run—and tell Amy I'm sorry I kept you." Stunned, I watched them rush to the stairs and yell over their shoulders, "Thanks, Rooooose."

I'd witnessed a miracle: students who were excited about a class that had once been feared—and who were now worried at the thought that they might miss a single moment of it. I later found out Amy had introduced many methods of collaborative learning in the class—including *Theater History Jeopardy*, role playing in debates, and much more. She managed to get actors to run joyfully toward this class, instead of—as Shakespeare wrote—"creeping like a snail unwillingly to school."

Sometimes, in a panicked response to losing important classroom time, we decide to skip to the end, or remove something important altogether. "I don't have time to do this activity, so I'll just put some notes on the board and you can all study at home." Or, "I'll assign you this extra chapter for homework, and though we won't have time to discuss it, it'll be on the test." Or even worse, we tell ourselves, "I'll just skip this lesson this semester. No one will know." The students *always* know, and wouldn't you all have a much better time with Yes And anyway?

*Party Challenge 4: Party Fouls: Unexpected and Disastrous Shortcomings in Class Materials and Student Results*

Teachers have all had this experience: we give a test, the day of the presentation arrives, the major paper comes due, or students have to demonstrate that they know how to take blood, solve major algebraic equations, or give a persuasive speech. And they blow it. As their instructor, holding a sad stack of red-ink-heavy papers, we have to let them know.

Solution: Again, an honest discussion is almost always better. "Many of you didn't do as well on this as you—and I—hoped. What do you think happened?" If you've created an open space of trust and exploration, you might be surprised to discover some students admitting to not studying enough or not knowing *how* to study.

Strategy: This can lead to a brief but important discussion about solutions. "The College Learning Center offers note-taking workshops to ensure you have enough information when you go home to study." "Practice the speech next time in the quad in front of a crowd. Report back about how it went. It'll work better than practicing in your room alone."

Through these discussions and suggestions, you reinforce that failure is a part of the process while also reassuring that there are solutions so they can work to improve and learn. And this, you may point out, is what they're paying all this money to do in the first place. Leading the students without judgment or blame creates an opportunity to fully explore issues and solutions for the future without losing your trusting, ensemble-driven environment.

*What Doesn't Work*

When there's a disastrous run-through of a play, directors find ways in their notes to suggest changes and improvements. If an actor isn't aware a run was disastrous, a director who immediately says, "You were really off tonight" doesn't help keep the ensemble connected and ready to trust their impulses, or one another, and take risks.

In the same way students might genuinely believe they aced a test and turn ashen when they read "54" atop the page while you say, "You guys really blew it." This, of course, is all true, but it breaks the trust in the room and inhibits how they respond to your ideas going forward. Our students now have less confidence, place blame, or feel separate from those in the room who might have done well. And we've lost our ensemble.

*A Note on Textbooks.* Sometimes the problem is the required text for a class. You don't always have a choice or even a voice in how it is chosen. Many dangers exist in a poorly written or poorly selected textbook. The content is woefully out of date. Chapters contain only male pronouns throughout. The three-hundred-page book contains a single chapter on the primary focus of the course, and the rest of this $275 book has material the students don't need.

Throughout their career, theater directors eventually work on a less-than-stellar script. The characters are thin, the structure is off-putting, or the plot doesn't entirely make sense. The solution? Admit it, and then make it better by building on the nuggets of good things that *are* there. In the classroom, you agree that the textbook is pretty bad. Offer them solutions. "I'll only assign parts of chapters I think you should know." "We'll read through the problematic chapters together and identify what's helpful and make fun of how bad the other stuff is."

Usually we know before a course begins if the textbook is a problem. This gives us a chance to change our approach. We can lean less on the text throughout the course, but textbooks are expensive, and if we're required to use it, it's unethical to make the students spend money on something that will remain at the bottom of a bookbag. Instead, discuss the shortcomings of the book. Let the students bring it up.

- "You said the thesis was the most important part of the outline, but the book doesn't even mention it in the chapter on how to outline!" "The writer is supposed to be discussing the conditions of slaughterhouses in turn-of-the-century America, but it feels like he keeps suggesting we shouldn't eat meat." Our response might be, "Clearly, this author doesn't understand the importance of thesis statements as well as you do. Well done!" And "You're right! The author seems to have a private agenda. Can we identify other areas that prove this?"
- These moments can also allow you to augment a textbook that is lacking with better online resources. Providing web links for students to explore as an answer to a collective problem often makes for an interesting archeology dig for the student: "This makes so much more sense than the book because . . ."

Sometimes, of course, it isn't the textbook so much as a student's understanding of what they read and how they can connect the reading to the class discussions and activities. A student says, "The textbook says settlers attacking Native Americans was the only reason Native Americans lost their lives." You know there's a whole section on the role of disease the student must have skimmed or missed. Often, they just need their memory jogged. "What else might have been a problem for Native Americans when they met the settlers? Do you remember from our discussion of the Louisiana Purchase?"

It's most important to explore ways to overcome both out-of-date materials or a student's lack of experience reading them so they won't have an opportunity to say, "I messed up that part because I didn't understand the reading."

*Party Challenge 5: Throwing Out the Troublemaker — Behavioral/Discipline Issues in the Classroom*

A discipline issue is a discipline issue no matter where you are. Sometimes it's beyond moments of unpreparedness or mistakes. Sometimes students bring their problems to a classroom. Outbursts. Distractions. The results can be far more negative and harmful to the lesson, to the room, and to the ensemble.

---

**Rose**

I once directed a show with a terrific cast; however, one actor was insecure about his work; let's call him Lou. Lou had been generous and collaborative throughout rehearsals, but a few days before we opened, he began to get defensive with the cast—and with me. I could tell that Lou was putting extra pressure on himself for not being "further ahead" of the other actors (he had a pretty healthy ego), and he didn't like hearing that he still had adjustments to make.

I was giving notes at a dress rehearsal, and Lou suddenly huffed, rolled his eyes, and said, "I don't need any more notes. I'm done." There was a moment of stunned silence; to this day, the stage manager tells me it took all of his willpower not to thump Lou with the production book. I had to make a quick decision on how to handle it.

I said—not unkindly—"Okay. No more notes then for you, Lou." I scanned the page for my next note, and muttered, "Nope, that's Lou . . . Lou . . . ah! Julie, when you make your entrance in scene 2, could you bring the sweater in with you instead of exiting to get it in scene 3? Thanks. Now, Lou . . . Lou . . . ah, Sabrina! When you . . ." And so on.

I acknowledged I had notes for Lou, included him, but made a point not to share his notes. I instinctively gambled Lou would become curious, then begin to feel left out, then observe the rest of the cast respond positively to the feedback, and would then want to know what his notes were.

The next night, when Lou was sure he was out of earshot of everyone else, he grudgingly said, "You know, if you have a few notes for me tonight, you can give them to me." I was cordial and said, "Well, Lou, I don't know what you mean by a 'few.' The notes I take are the notes I see—I either give you all like everyone else, or none." I saw his face start to twist a bit and said, "We're in good shape; I can't imagine there'll be many." He seemed to relax and said, "OK."

He ended up being wonderful in the role—as I trusted he would— but he clearly didn't trust himself, or me in that moment. I could have focused on his rudeness, which would have distracted the entire cast

> and put the focus on everything except the play. Instead, I made Lou want to be part of the group again—he had no one left to be angry at except himself, and because there was no Big Actor/Director confrontation, nothing haunted the production. The show was a success—I never worked with Lou again, but I always wished him well.

Colleges and universities often have behavioral remedies in place. Deans to visit. Parents to call. Students are suspended or expelled. Sometimes a teacher-centric response is needed.

- Solution to negative, distracting outbursts: "Your outbursts are pulling attention from the ensemble, from me, and from the lesson. This needs to be about all of us, and you're making it about you." Using theater, you've removed the idea of the "teacher as authority figure against whom to rebel." You've created a trusting, collaborative environment. Often, students exhibit repeated negative behavior to get a laugh from classmates or as a good defense mechanism from whatever else is going on in their lives. When the student realizes this behavior is upsetting not only you but also the balance of the class, the student will question their own behavior in the eyes of the ensemble, rather than seeing a "me versus him" scenario.
- Solution to not listening, bad attitude, and refusal to participate: When an actor is behaving badly in rehearsal, we try to redirect that behavior by giving them a new action, raising their status by asking them to help us with an imagined problem, or giving them an exercise that illustrates their bad behavior to them. This creates an opportunity for the actor—and your student—to discover their unhelpful behavior and puts them on a journey of improving themselves. With your troublesome student, you can try several methods, with the goal of creating increased empathy, for themselves, their peers, and you.
- For example, let the "punishment" for their bad behavior be a special assignment to design an exercise or "lesson" for the class to do at the next session. And they need to "teach" it. Whether they take advantage of the opportunity or not will give you insight into their behavior. Do they come in with an exercise that resonates with the material you've been covering, shows that they *have* been listening, and includes their peers in a positive way? Are they invested in their action *to instruct, to lead*, and *to guide*? Does the troubled student get frustrated if their peers are joking about their "substitute" teacher? (This could be a *good* thing for their empathy levels.) Or have they blown off the assignment and brought in something that shows carelessness, or even malice?

- Solution to an overenthusiastic student who volunteers for everything, stepping on other students' responses and impulses: "When we do activities, I love that you get excited and always volunteer. How can we use that to help some of the others get as many opportunities to engage and grow as you so enjoy doing?" You've become wonderfully conspiratorial in that you *need* their help. For example, ask such a student to introduce a theater game of his own. Add to the rules to make it work for you but give them a creative outlet in the moment that will show how you value that energy—when it's directed in a helpful way.

Of course, only when the student *consistently* responds with bitterness, disrespect, and one-word answers should we consider removal—not the occasional bad day. Sometimes a student is rude and short with you *once*. You go home and have to spend a little extra time trying to shake it off. What you don't know is that the student does the same thing. Regret is a powerful drive, and given time to stew, they will hopefully come in the next day and seek guidance. If they don't, one of those one-on-one office visits might be necessary to give them the privacy and space they need to come forward with an explanation or apology.

It's rare (hopefully) to have to remove a student, but this actually benefits the class, because the problem student was killing the ensemble. The student will need to be helped by someone who is better equipped for whatever is truly ailing them. We can't solve every problem our students have, and if we try to do so beyond a reasonable point, we end up potentially making the situation worse, not just for the student but also for the whole class.

By removing a student and pointing them toward someone or something that may actually help, the ensemble will be greatly improved, bonded, and connected, and you're a better leader for seeing that need and acting on it. Removing a student can be upsetting to the rest of the class. You can't reveal details of their removal, but you can discuss how your students feel, address those feelings, and try activities to return them to their quest of getting to the end of the story.

For example, play the improv game you did at the beginning of the semester. The ensemble will see what is needed now that the problem has been resolved and what they can do to fill the hole left by the former classmate.

Often the person who leaves, though they may have been distracting and inappropriate, did contribute something helpful to the group. He'd guess at an answer to a question when no one else would. He'd give an honest assessment of a video or reading that would encourage others to share openly and honestly.

Now that he's gone, the other students in the ensemble will note that absence as much as you do. But with your encouragement—and in the collaborative environment all of you have created—your students will begin to contribute in his stead. They'll notice the pause, his absence, and almost as a single breathing entity, they'll begin to work harder to answer those questions: to volunteer first or to begin with an honest response to a question. Your ensemble will be stronger than ever, fostering trust in the director.

## TRUSTING THE DIRECTOR

Using theater as a guiding philosophical approach means trusting your students to engage in the techniques you've used to create a collaborative environment. Sometimes, though, you may feel you're walking a tightrope without a net. What if the students don't engage? What if I can't do this? Directors go through this all the time. What if I've misunderstood some aspect of the story? What if the actors don't like the subject matter, or are playing unlikeable characters?

Just as you've learned to trust your students and give them an environment in which *they* can trust and take risks, you have to remind yourself to inhabit that same environment. You're the leader of the ensemble, and as such they're looking to you to guide them. They're not looking at you for every answer; you're all working together for those. Trust yourself, take a risk, and see what happens. You'll find you're already prepared to handle the possibilities that are waiting for you, whether they're well documented or new and unexpected. It's part of what makes you a member of the ensemble as well as its leader.

And when challenges arise? You're well equipped to meet those challenges as a theater director would: collaboratively. The environment you've created means you're not doing this alone. You're prepared to address these challenges together; with the help of these students, you've developed into risk-taking, life-engaging storytellers prepared to overcome obstacles with, and for, the group.

*Chapter Seven*

# Your Stage in Action

*Using Theater to Teach Writing*

Regardless of your discipline, you and your curriculum can now benefit from applying theater techniques in the classroom. You may be wondering how to adapt these techniques to your subject area. One aspect of education crosses all disciplines: good writing is essential in every major. Theater is the energizing boost your students and you need to create powerful, effective writing. This chapter will explore how you can use theater techniques to teach students some much-needed writing skills, regardless of your area of expertise.

Our students' previous experience with writing and composition classes in high school and middle school varies widely; some are well prepared, while others struggle to hit the bottom of the second page of a two-page assignment without repeating the word "very" too many times.

High school English teachers are working hard to prepare their students for the writing rigors of colleges and universities. However, when institutions focus on developing curriculum to meet the requirements of *only* standardized tests that determine budgets and meet graduation rates, writing can be forgotten. At one California high school, when a state representative from the Department of Education visited an English class, he told the teacher to give less attention to writing and more to multiple-choice assignments. The teacher was told, "The test has no writing component" (Rizga 2011).

Yet standardized tests can't possibly measure the power of writing, the ability to communicate complex and interesting concepts, or the nuanced, analytical ideas our students might have. According to Bronwyn T. Williams's article "Standardized Students: The Problems with Writing for Tests Instead of People," "When work is written only to be assessed rather than to communicate ideas, the activity becomes more about ensuring that certain qualities are present (e.g., the use of examples, the complexity of sentences, transition, vocabulary) regardless of the overall effect of the piece of writing" (2005).

Once students find themselves in the college classroom with little understanding of the power and importance of how to express themselves in writing in academic or professional settings, they struggle to meet the standards of freshman writing classes, much less any of the requirements of their program. How can you make certain your students are equipped to dive into the writing and research process required by your assignments and able to use writing to engage in their academic and eventual professional lives?

Theater, of course.

Even the lonely process of writing can model the collaborative nature of theater. Lively class discussions about a writing or research assignment can energize students before they begin to shape their outlines and first drafts. They'll make discoveries during workshops or peer reviews, when they get to take a break from their lonely cocoon of writing and play with others. They'll reshape and strengthen their drafts, like tiny rehearsals for an eventual production of an essay.

Through imagination, listening, and saying Yes And to each step of the writing and research process, your students will begin to see writing, regardless of the course, as an opportunity to engage one another and entertain an audience from their personal stage.

## TEXT MESSAGE PEOPLE IN A COVER LETTER WORLD

Our students of the last ten to fifteen years spend more time writing than the students ten to fifteen years before them. They might not spend that time on essays, poetry, literary criticism, or science hypotheses, but they do communicate with acronyms, emojis, and memes. It's often the primary way our students "talk" with one another when not in our classroom. They'd rather send a text or email, or post a social media message than pick up a phone or speak to someone face to face.

As Christian De Matteo teaches in his writing lab lesson "Text Message People in a Cover Letter World," the skills used in those types of messages—clever acronyms and quick phrases as they drive across town or sneak out a message under their desk—aren't the same skills they'll need to communicate in the professional world. Whether they're in accounting, medical assisting, or art and design, our students are going to have to express themselves clearly in writing.

At the very least, they'll need a cover letter and résumé to try to get a job. Yet some students aren't being given the foundation to build their writing skills, and by the time they show up in our classroom, they're unprepared to effectively communicate with us on any assignments that require them to prove their understanding of course material in writing.

By using the newfound techniques you've learned through this book, you can guide your students to improve their overall writing techniques and help them develop a process that will nurture their contributions. This will leave them better able to engage a potential employer or confidently request that big raise from their current job.

## THE FIRST DRAFT: USING YES AND

Earlier chapters discuss how theater practitioners use the improvisation philosophy of Yes And. Yes And encourages actors to make any choice in rehearsal as a first step in a longer process, so that directors and actors can work on sculpting the final version of the story out of that initial choice. If an actor won't make a choice, there's not much story that can be told.

Writing a first draft is like that first step in the rehearsal process. Whether outlining the structure and ideas first or jumping right into the first draft, many students will stare at the blank screen not knowing how to start the process of this three-page essay on why smoking is bad for you. Eventually, some students will shut down the program, tell themselves they'll get to it later, and check out what's going on in social media.

Just as in rehearsal, a writer needs to say Yes And to the writing process. Their fear of what may happen when they write displays itself as the same little voice in the head that an actor hears. "What if I make a choice, and it sounds stupid? Or I think it's good and put myself out there and no one likes it?" If we teach our students to say Yes And to their first draft, they'll bypass this voice and produce *something*, even if it's not yet the best version of it.

In rehearsals, an actor's choice isn't necessarily the best one for the eventual performance. An actor, Angela, might read a scene in which she has to console her grieving friend over the loss of a dog, and might decide to deliver the line "He was a great dog, Bill" with sarcasm that makes Bill agonize more over the loss instead of beginning to heal.

The director asks Angela, "Why'd you make that choice? What are you doing here?" The director and Angela work together and eventually land on a more sympathy-rich reading that will help Angela get what she wants from Bill (to open up about his loss instead of holding it all in). This allows Bill to release his grief about his beloved dog and, hopefully, give the audience a nice, tear-filled emotional reaction.

What most directors can't do in response to an actor's first choice—because most actors aren't helped by it—is say, "That's wrong. Start over with this scene, throw out all your ideas, and try something else." This would ruin the relationship between the director and actor, kill the trust the actor has placed in the director, and make it harder than ever for the actor to find something meaningful in the scene. Like actors, our students need Permission to Screw Up.

### Mike

A few years ago I started teaching for a liberal arts program aimed at professional dancers. Often, ballet dancers will go right from grade school to a professional ballet company, and then they retire sometime in their late twenties or early thirties—and need to make a living.

I would teach these students in a college writing class that was also the first class they'd take in the program. At the beginning, they were scared of the class, this college lifestyle, what a degree would mean for their future, and what their lives would be like when they couldn't dance anymore. A part of my job, in addition to teaching them various academic writing techniques, was to orient them to college and, in a way, show them that everything was going to be okay.

They were some of the most disciplined, hardest-working students I ever knew. They learned those characteristics as dancers. You don't make it in the New York City Ballet without working really hard, giving up on sleep and food and free time, and developing a strong sense of self-discipline. Applied to a college degree plan, they could easily be successful and often accomplished their degrees with a 4.0.

But in that early writing class, they showed up and strove for perfection, only to discover that their first draft wasn't perfect. They thought it should be. They thought that if they stayed up all night writing and rereading their essays that they'd hand them in and get As. When I told them only a first draft was due, and they could just write it and bring it to class, they were shocked.

Eventually, I came up with the phrase "You have Permission to Screw Up." In the world of dance, no one ever told them that before. In writing, it's a necessary part of the process. Screw up, and figure out how to fix it. And that helps them learn stronger skills for the next time they do it, so they're not just "fixing" but also starting with something better to begin with—and that helps them grow!

By the midpoint of the class, these dancers fully embraced the idea. Overwhelmed by the unknown of their future, a new college lifestyle, and a thick regimen of college assignments, these students welcomed those first draft assignments. They worked hard on each one, but they took my feedback, and the feedback of their classmates, with grace and joy, and used it to improve their work every time. Some of the greatest essays I ever read came from dance students who had no experience in writing, because they accepted, and used, the Permission to Screw Up.

## PERMISSION TO SCREW UP

Actors need this understanding in the rehearsal process all the time: permission to make choices that won't be judged, or to map out different possibilities within the space of the play so they get to know their characters, partners, and those relationships. Writers need to be able to do the same: to get to know their topic, to try proving their thesis with the initial ideas, to see what works and what doesn't work, and to begin to understand how to adjust it in the second draft.

When you assign your students an outline or first draft, give them Permission to Screw Up. This will reduce the anxiety they may feel at having to "get it right" in the outline or in their first attempts at the essay. An outline is meant to be a structured map in which they can explore how their ideas fit together. A first draft is just as exploratory: following the map of their outline to *begin* the journey of the writing process, exploring how the story of their essay works from introduction to conclusion.

Make sure students save the heavy lifting for the revision process. Too often, students think editing is finding missing or extraneous commas or, maybe, a sentence fragment. Revising is about the entire document, making their writing clearer, more interesting, and yes, grammatically correct. Students will begin to realize they can devote more time and energy to letting their ideas flow and then go back to see if they've captured those ideas as intended. They'll set aside grammatical and structural perfection until a later revision part of the process.

When students hear this, they don't always believe it, or can't convince themselves to divide up the editorial process. As in theater, teachers need to reinforce the joy of exploration and, once again, reassure students that failure is part of that journey. Remind your students of the following:

- There are no wrong answers.
- Try to express yourselves the best you can.
- Outline a basic plan of how to proceed and follow it; if you have an impulse to change your outline, do it. You drew this map, but if you find a stronger way to make your point, or a more interesting journey you could take the reader on, explore that impulse. You'll have plenty of opportunities to try different choices while outlining and drafting, and even during

the research part of the process. (More on applying research later in this chapter.)
- As you write the first draft, if you make grammar mistakes, keep going. It's okay the first time through.
- Don't stop until you have at least the classic five-paragraph essay with an introduction, body, and conclusion. If four out of five paragraphs are bad, that's okay. If you followed your outline but you now have some different ideas, make note of them. Conversely, if you veered from your outline throughout the drafting process and you're worried about it, note the areas in which you changed course and what pulled you in that new direction.
- Later, during the revision process, look at the notes regarding how closely you followed your outline and ask yourself, What stronger choices could I make? Why did I veer off course, and how did that improve the essay? How could it still be improved?

If you've been including some of the theater exercises previously suggested, ask students, Was veering off course something that often happens, or have you been taking more risks to make changes since doing some of the theater exercises? That is, how might their practice of learning and exploring be changing as a result of doing more collaborative exercises?

The drafting process can be terrible. Students will spend part of the process doubting that they'll use any of the words they put down, and the rest of it sure it's all awful and a waste of time. But the real drive of drafting, using an outline or not, comes with the ability to keep going. Their ability to keep going comes from *your* encouragement with Yes And, when they realize they have Permission to Screw Up. Once they look back on the complete draft, it might not be great, but it'll be better than what it felt like as they were doing it—and a whole lot better than having nothing at all.

## USING YOUR SCENE PARTNER TO WORKSHOP

Just as an actor works with their scene partner and collaborates with a director, a student with a first draft needs to work with partners or tutors to get to the second draft. Every major published document—book, law, comic book, or religious text—has had at least one other pair of eyes on it. The one you're reading right now has not only been written with a sturdy back-and-forth between cowriters but also had a valuable team of readers and insightful editors who have shaped and formed the result.

Our best writers eventually leave the cocoon of their writing space to receive helpful feedback and ideas from others. We expect them to do this. It's how we have great literature, life-saving journalism, and all-important texts on how to use theater in nontheater classrooms.

Why then do we assign students a paper and expect them to go into their own cocoons, write it, and hand it in? A single writing workshop can elevate a student's draft to something that you might even enjoy reading. But how do workshops work? How do we help them be open to feedback from others and guide them in giving their partners feedback that's constructive and not *destructive*?

We do this by treating one another as acting partners. Chapter 5 discussed how you can be an acting partner with your students and motivate them to collaborate with one another:

- Yes And
- Make Your Partner Look Good
- Follow the Fear
- Dare to Make the Obvious Choice
- Take Care of and Support your Partner

Your students are ready to explore these techniques in the context of exchanging feedback in a writing workshop. Have them bring in their drafts, partner up with someone, and exchange papers. Create a random system (e.g., count off 1–2–3–4, all 1s partner with a 3, all 2s with a 4, and so on); this way, a student doesn't immediately choose a best pal who might not be honest with feedback, or who may feel weird giving *any* feedback to their friend.

Give them a series of questions to ask one another, and later, when they're more familiar with the process, they may create questions of their own. Keep the questions direct, relevant, and helpful, and they'll use them to support one another and their writing. For example:

- What moments from the draft were meaningful, surprising, memorable, or evocative? Ask them to avoid using "like" or "dislike." Those words can create a state of mind where the writer is only listening for compliments or criticisms; neither allows them to be open to *all* feedback. Giving students specific adjectives related to interesting writing will help them focus on those elements and look for more than grammar and typos.
- What's your favorite passage from the paper? This helps students stay present, listen, and respond. They must have *something* to say, a personal take or response. In theater terminology, there's something at stake. How would the student feel if their partner read their paper and said absolutely nothing about their hard work?
- When were you confused? In theater, we ask actors to get more specific. Instead of telling them to act sad, we ask, "What action can you do that could evoke the feeling of sadness in your partner?" In writing, you can

ask a partner, "Can you get more specific with this paragraph on the emotional impact of smoking? With your thesis statement?"
- Did the paper ever slow down or get lost in itself? Were there too many sentences devoted to one point and not enough to another? When directors find themselves disconnected from a scene in rehearsal, not paying attention to actors working through a scene, it's usually a sign the audience will be disconnected as well. We explore what we can do to make it connect more, to us, to the scene partners, and to the audience.

If a workshop partner finds herself drifting off while she's reading, it might be not because the paper's about motorcycle repair and she doesn't care about motorcycles but because the writer isn't pulling the reader in. Has the writer found a personal connection to the topic? What do they uniquely have to say about motorcycles?

This is the equivalent of an actor playing Hamlet who hasn't personally invested in their choices; the audience doesn't believe them as Hamlet because the actor doesn't believe what they're doing. It's the same for your student's writing. Perhaps the sentences are too vague, which may indicate the author feels vague about the subject. Regardless of the reason, it's a good time to discuss what the issue might be, giving the writer valuable information to help him on the second draft.
- Did the writer prove the thesis? This is the million-dollar question in writing. A writer must be able to state in a sentence what it is they're going to prove in the essay and then spend the rest of the essay using expression, argument, and evidence to prove it. Often, it's a complicated issue that's hard to understand, and a deeper exploration will help clarify and revise.

- Does each point in the body of the essay contribute to the thesis and the unity of the paper itself?
- What points could be stronger, expanded on, and buoyed by research?
- Could the thesis statement itself be tightened or rewritten to avoid having to rewrite a substantial chunk of the paper?

In theater, directors don't always know what we have; it's a forest for the trees situation. We rehearse a play for weeks, and eventually we need friends or colleagues to watch a run of the play and give us feedback. Often directors will have questions for those colleagues. "What would you say the theme is after watching the rehearsal tonight?" The answer might not be what we had in mind, but it will help us strengthen the play so that, when it goes before an audience, they'll react the way we hope for.

Make sure your students know that constructive feedback must keep the focus on the work, not on the creator. That will reinforce their mutual support as a team: "We're learning this together at the same time; here's what I noticed in your essay that could be strengthened, based on what we both just learned in class."

You can always apply techniques from Liz Lerman's book (with John Borstel) *Critical Response Process: A Method for Getting Useful Feedback on Anything from Dance to Dessert* (2003). Lerman is a choreographer who devised this process with her dance company when they would create new work. This four-step process keeps the feedback focused on the work that's being developed, and not on the artist themselves:

1. Discuss moments that were meaningful, surprising, memorable, and moving. Start the ball rolling by asking, "What is meaningful to you in the draft you've just read?" Remind them to avoid words such as "liked," "disliked," "better," and "worse"; focus on the power and clarity of the work being communicated, not a "review" of it. This helps the writer begin the process knowing that their work has meaning, and value, to another person.
2. The writer asks neutral questions about an aspect of the essay they're struggling with: "Was the relationship between smoking and the release of dopamine in the brain clear to you?" (not "Did you like the part about dopamine?", which is fishing for compliments rather than for constructive feedback). The responders should try to use the neutral language provided by the writer in their response: "No, it wasn't clear. And, here's an example of when I got confused…" In this way, any student who may have wanted to respond but held back out of fear of hurting the writer's feelings has been given an "invitation" to offer their responses.
3. Responders are now permitted to ask neutral questions of the writer. Instead of saying, "Why is it so long?" (which has the embedded opinion of "the essay is way too long"), they ask a neutral question, "Can you tell me the most important ideas you want me to get and where that's happening in this essay?"
4. When the partners accept all ideas and ask and answer questions neutrally, and honestly, you can then open it up for opinions, which the partners should ask permission to give. "I have an opinion about your paragraph on the emotional impact of smoking. Would you like to hear it?" This allows each writer to have agency; they know best how much critique they can process at that moment. If steps 1 to 3 have been honored, they'll also be more open to critical feedback, knowing the focus is placed firmly on the work, and not on them as the creator of the work.

*A Note on Time*: Unless you're teaching an English composition class, you may not have time for multiple drafts. There's a lot to cover in an American history class on "The Revolutionary War to Today," and probably very little time for multiple revisions and workshops. But you *can* embed first drafts into the homework schedule.

Have students bring their drafts to class or your office hours so you can spot-check. Give the students a group project in which they meet outside of class, exchange papers, and give each other feedback. Have the class record a journal discussing what they discovered in the revision process, or refer them to the college's learning center for tutoring as part of the assignment.

If you can afford the extra step and it won't take away from precious classroom time, you'll get better papers while at the same time teaching the students how to write and edit. Without fear or judgment, they'll have an easier time getting their words out so they can begin to play, explore, and become more adventurous, skilled writers.

Writing, after all, isn't just an academic process. It's a creative one, full of all the connective artistic and emotional tissue that makes writing powerful. When you create an emotionally safe space where students feel open to review and work together on their ideas, they'll write with a clearer and more productive understanding of the next steps in the process. They'll also have gained confidence in personally investing in their topic: *they* weren't critiqued, their *work* was.

A much lonelier, and sometimes far less emotionally safe, process for many students is doing research for a paper. Hours alone at the library or in front of the computer, staring at academic databases full of scholarly articles, can drive many students deeper into their fear and cease the writing process altogether. Again, using collaborative techniques to motivate this next step can encourage your students to explore their ideas and take ownership of their writing.

## RESEARCH PAPERS, DISCOVERY, AND THE NEED FOR TRUST, OVERCOMING FEAR, AND TAKING RISKS

Research is an integral part of putting on a play. Though the artistic team might not write an essay at the end of the process, the play stands as a culmination of that research. The director is taking on *Romeo and Juliet*. He begins a deep dive into language, interpretation, previous versions, and events during the time period in which it was written as well as historical events in Verona, Italy.

He gets excited by this research and uses it throughout the production: he sends an article about a famous, fifteenth-century wealthy Italian family to the designers, who find historical photos of their palace and garments, which influences the set and costume design, which affects blocking, movement, and status choices. All of this research leads to thrilling revelations by the artists and makes the process more complete, more interesting, and far more fun to work on and engaging to an audience than if no research had been done at all.

Similarly, many students could benefit from considering research as a "process of discovery." Students must gather research and use it to develop and prove a thesis. To many of them, this is a long, boring process of reading and rereading books and articles, hoping they find the perfect quote to fit where they think it belongs in the paper. Sometimes they assume a quote is the one you *want* them to use, as if they're trying to fill in the blanks of your expectations.

Your goal is to get them to ask, "What research does my topic need?" "What am I interested in finding out about this?" "How can I prove what I believe to be true?"

Too often students choose a topic (or are assigned a topic) they have no interest in. They base their topics on something that sounds academic, that might be what the teacher wants instead of what *they* connect to. In psychology class, for example, Brianna chooses to write about how chemical reactions in the brain affects behavior. The only motivation pushing her on this journey: there's a paper due in a few weeks.

As she slogs across campus, she's thinking, *Uh. I'm so tired. I can't believe I have to spend the next three hours in the library.* Or even worse, she's developing anxiety over the breadth of the work research entails. "How can I possibly do all this research and write about it? It's too much." This paper and its research have been shaped for her as a required task, a means to an end, and that end is only a completed paper she doesn't have to worry about anymore.

In theater, actors have ownership of their roles, including any research about characters. When an actor playing Hamlet reads about the history of the play, or choices other actors have made, he's not doing it because a director assigned him additional work. He needs to create the role for himself—that is, to personalize his investment in the part.

The actor may start with "I love my dad, and like Hamlet, if anyone hurt him, I'd do everything in my power to make it right." He then explores further with research and asks, "How are Hamlet's circumstances different from mine? How does the time period, or his royal status, affect his ability to take action?" His research will affect the intriguing discoveries he makes and feed his motivation and enthusiasm that he uses throughout the process.

If your students feel they're going to bring to light and report something that only *they* can write, a story only *they* can tell, their investment in the project will be akin to that of an actor. The stakes will be theirs, tied to their need to learn more about their topic.

The research process is no longer about trying to fill in blanks they think match the teacher's expectations. They're now explorers setting out to report on what they find. When you assign research, you're encouraging your students to develop new ideas about their topic and come up with creative, interesting ways to express those ideas in writing. Students need *ownership* of the story they're researching.

For the psychology class example, the teacher used the concepts of scene partners explored in chapter 5 to engage his class in a discussion on how these chemical reactions have affected the students' behavior in the past. This discussion inspired Brianna's topic choice. It might still be tied to brain chemicals and their effect on behavior, but after the class, Brianna reflects on her recent heartbreak and finds much higher personal stakes in the topic of how chemical reactions in the brain and body lead people to fall in and out of love.

Like an actor who brings a piece of themselves to each role, she's "found a way in" to the subject and has a personal investment in exploring why she's experienced physiological and psychological changes since the breakup (perhaps anxiety, or sleeplessness). She's no longer doing research to find answers she thinks you expect but taking the subject matter you assigned and connecting it to answers she needs to find. Now, while she's walking across campus, she's thinking, *I don't know how I'm going to do this research, but I want to.*

Research topics vary from class to class, but encouraging students to find their connection to the topic—regardless of subject—is so important. If you assign a research paper and the students get to choose their topic, it's a little easier. "Find something you're interested in but don't know much about."

If it's a specific topic they have to investigate, encourage finding a connection to that topic, as Brianna does in the example. Research is a moment where you must step aside and let your students explore using the concepts you've shown them. The students conduct research through their unique personal lens, and they'll be attracted to some fact or detail that's important to *them*.

## OVERCOMING FEAR OF THE PROCESS

Of course, this power of discovery can be blocked if the student approaches the assignment with a sense of fear. "How can I possibly find all the information I need to prove my thesis? Finding it is going to take forever, and I don't have enough time to do it well."

Both fears are tied into the idea of self-doubt. Students don't yet see a personal connection to the material. "I'm not good enough to do this. I don't know what the teacher wants or what I can bring to this topic. I'm going to fail." They're shortchanging themselves, and there's room in every assignment to check in: "Why might this take forever? Why wouldn't you be good enough? Learning how to do this is part of the point!" Just as with their fear of screwing up, and the fear of showing others their work, encourage them to define and meet the fear:

- Finding information to prove a thesis

  - If a director decides to direct *Hamlet*, she'd have to research its language and history. This is the equivalent of a teacher handing a student a list of research topics they *have* to do. But the director *also* chooses to set the play on the moon; she made that decision because she has a deep personal interest in space travel and realized that imagining being on another planet resonated with the depth of the isolation and alienation that Hamlet feels. She then gets to do research tied to her own idea of, and personal connection to, the project.

    She'd research the moon, space, an environment that lacks oxygen, and how gravity might affect the body and brain chemicals associated with revenge, fear, and the need to take action. This additional research connects to the director's personal stakes and adds to the thrill of the process. Research provides additional truths and adds richness to the world of the play, the story, and the essay. Without it, the process itself would be empty, confusing, and boring.
  - Send the student to begin their research journey with the intent of discovering ideas related to their personal thoughts and questions, rather than trying to fit specific quotes into a narrow, possibly misconceived thesis.

    - If a student has an idea about a thesis and *not* a strongly held belief they're intent on proving, the assignment becomes an exciting process of unearthing details related to their topic. They can now connect those details to developing their specific thesis.
    - When Brianna, the student suffering from heartbreak, begins with "Love is kicked off by something in the brain and I've heard that pheromones play a role . . . but what role is it?" instead of a too-specific "Love is caused by chemicals in the brain that are set off by pheromones," the assignment becomes *her* idea, rather than a task she's forced to do.

- "This is gonna take forever and is gonna be boring."

  - The student now has a goal—figure out what causes love—that is tied to learning and "aha!" moments, and in this story of research, the student has an obstacle: the fear of not being able to do this. They now have reinforcement from their workshop partners and know that if they screw up, it's part of learning. They're more willing to allow for failure, to prepare themselves for obstacles. They've been given agency over the assignment, and you've revealed to them a path to follow, designed to allow for new and exciting territory.

- What better way to inspire students to express their knowledge than by giving them ownership over it and keeping them invested in the project for personal *and* academic reasons? Since the frame of the story is now "Journey to discover what causes love," Brianna has a need to fulfill. "I need to figure this out, and once I do, I need to use my discoveries to teach someone else what I learned. And to recognize the symptoms the next time *I* fall in love."
- The stakes go from "I need to get this done and get a good grade" to "I'm learning a lot about the chemical nature of love, but I need to frame it in a three-page paper and convince the reader that what I've found is true and get them to care about it like I now do."
- What if Brianna has a friend who had also fallen in love, was miserable, and didn't understand why? Even while framing the paper, Brianna has a heap of new information to help herself and her friend. They make revelations that benefit them in mutual support and a newfound understanding of their shared experience.
- Give your students checkpoints if their newfound agency (instilled in them by the techniques discussed in this book) doesn't quite cure them of their fear about the time this project could take. Be the Gandalf to their lonely journey through Mordor, or their director who watches the run of an important scene.
- Ask them to bring in two compelling pieces of research they found and explain to you and the class why it will help them tell the story. Then do it again a week later. Have them bring in a draft of the first three paragraphs, including properly cited research. You could even ask them to bring in a full draft of the research paper itself and discuss what pieces of the story are missing, and give them some new and unexpected sources that might help them prove that thesis.

That doesn't necessarily mean the research process will be as thrilling as an *Indiana Jones* movie, but in giving the student a goal that's tied to a personal journey, you increase the chances that she will invest in her topic, her research, and her writing. And when a student is interested in what they're doing, you're more likely to be interested in the results.

They may still need time with a draft, help with grammar, and some feedback from a workshop partner. Even in doing that, it's *their own* process, and a goal to communicate with all readers, rather than trying to fulfill a framework for the teacher alone, at the end of which is a grade.

## CONCLUSION: GIVING STUDENTS THE CONFIDENCE AND TECHNIQUES TO WRITE

By reshaping their writing habits and experiences, your students will begin to look at the writing process in a new, collaborative light. Much like when you encourage your students to conquer their fear and engage in new and invigorating learning activities, their writing habits will need some attention. Their individual voice will begin to take shape in their writing.

They will approach other writing endeavors using the same process, making similar discoveries and snagging their readers with their unique creative voice. Cover letters will begin to reveal their interesting personalities and make potential employers think, *I want to call this person.* Colleagues and clients will read their business emails because they'll tell an engaging story using language that draws in the reader, rather than the drab "to whom it may concern." Letters and emails to editors, to customer service departments, and even to friends and family will gather extra attention and enthusiasm, especially in this day of emojis and memes.

And their readers—potential or current employers, colleagues, and clients—will notice them for that personality, will remember who they are and what they represent, and will want to communicate with them. They'll get the interview, secure the raise, win over the client, or help a member of the sales team. Overall, good, invested, personality-based writers become much-wanted parts of the job market.

Beyond their careers, they'll find a great circle of possibility in applying these ideas. These concepts will make them stronger and more empathetic humans, better able to navigate their families, friendships, and romances—their new and exciting ensembles—as well as all the successes and failures they will undoubtedly encounter throughout their lives.

It all starts in your classroom. By applying the concepts and techniques discussed in this book, your students take risks, act on impulses, and use their discoveries to become creative writers, and their readers will engage with them in a way that's far too rare now. You will have transformed your classroom to a stage where the play is well written, the performances are collaborative and compelling, and the audience is affected by the clear and strong communication of the story.

# Conclusion

## *The Curtain Call*

In theater, all the training, work, rehearsals, and preparation eventually build to the performance, and the collaborative circle is complete. The last of our collaborators—the audience—joins us, and together we have the profound experience of a story shared together. Every skill and concept coalesces into that experience—and then the curtain closes. The cast steps out, the audience applauds, and everyone gets back in their cars or catches their trains. Eventually, the show closes, the ensemble parts ways, and each individual finds and forms *new* ensembles that take exciting, previously unexplored journeys together.

Our students will earn the grade, walk across the stage at graduation, and after a few photographs, they'll get to their cars or catch their trains. And we, their scene partners, their director, their onetime collaborator, will have hopefully given them the knowledge they need to successfully get and perform well at a job in their desired field.

Their performance at that job will have been influenced by all the concepts we've taught them: Yes And, listening, learning through play, empathy, risk taking, trusting their impulses and choices, trusting others, and trusting themselves.

And what about your job? You'll continue to use theater to influence the craft of teaching as you guide your new collaborators, year after year. You'll make new discoveries, even as your students do, and together you'll continue to develop the story of your subject area, of each lesson you plan and teach, of the shared stage that is your classroom.

It all starts with you and a group of nervous, uncertain students standing in a circle as the water pipe in the back slowly drips into a bucket. One of them looks another in the eye, gestures, and says, "Zing!"

Their—and your—journey begins.

# Appendix A

## *Blind Offers (via Keith Johnstone in* Impro*)*

**Focus:** Commitment, listening, nonverbal communication, taking responsibility for a partner, trust, observation, Yes And
**How to:** Two partners, A and B (group observes)

- Partner A makes a spontaneous, intentionless physical offer/gesture to Partner B, and holds it. Encourage them not to plan ahead.
- Partner B immediately responds with their own physical, nonverbal response to A's offer, and holds it.
- At the moment of the dual hold, partner A says "thank you," and then both release to neutral.

    - For example: Partner A might arch their back forward, with both arms outstretched in front of them with palms down, and then hold. B might respond by stretching their arms forward with palms up, directly underneath the palms of A, and then hold that position. Both hold that unified image for a beat, and then A says "thank you."

- Partner B makes a spontaneous, intentionless physical offer/gesture to A, and so forth.
- Be mindful that partners take their time with the "thank you."
- Have them take at least three turns each. The offers should be spontaneous, abstract, and again, without planning.
- The goal is not to tell a literal story but to make a fully committed offer that is accepted every time. For example, if A points their finger at B, B needn't hold up their hands as if they're being robbed.

## Benefits:

- Emphasizes that *every* offer (their ideas and responses in classroom discussions, group projects, or answering prompts from the teacher) will be accepted, that a partner will *always* discover a response to each offer, and that the offer—and the individual—is valued, and is "enough."
- Reduces fear of rejection and helps students with harsh self-judgment.
- Nurtures physical awareness, expression, and confidence through exploring ideas and impulses with the body. When students participate in class, whether from their seats or in front of the room, they can be self-conscious about physical expression and appearance. In the digital age where anyone can swiftly edit or delete a photo that's perceived as unflattering, physical spontaneity is often inhibited in pursuit of a "perfect" look.
- Encourages holistic listening and creates an understanding of the essential building blocks of trust that comes from true listen/response between partners.

## Discussion:

- How did you feel when you were asked to lead a round? Responsible? Fearful? Trusted? Does that relate to how you participate in class?
- How did you feel when you observed your partner's response to your offer? (When partners respond every single time, the Yes And element nurtures risk taking.)
- Describe how the "thank you" felt. What's the equivalent of that in classroom exchanges?
- What would it mean if you thought someone was going to say "thank you" every time you offered an idea or suggestion? How can you apply these discoveries to our class?

# Appendix B

## *Come Join Me (via Viola Spolin)*

**Focus:** Awareness, agreement, collaboration, commitment, imagination, observation, specificity, Yes And
**How to:** The group stands off to one side of the playing area.

- Ask for a volunteer to begin; they should enter the playing area and start a nonverbal, independent physical activity that establishes a specific environment. Any prop or furniture items should be mimed.
- As other ensemble members recognize the action and the environment, *one at a time*, they should enter and make their own contribution to the environment through an activity—and a role—that would also be found in that environment. For example, if the person who initiates is working out on a treadmill, the next person may enter and be a custodian, the next person creates a front desk for gym membership, and so on.
- Remind students to play humans, not animals, trees, or furniture (you can change that later on after students become familiar with the benefits of the exercise).
- Once others join, the scenario *can* become verbal, but it's not required. What you *don't* want is the person initiating to announce, "It sure is hot in this *beauty salon*." Their specific physical activity should communicate that.
- Side-coach to ensure that students are entering one at a time, so they can observe what each individual is contributing to the environment. If someone establishes a school playground, and eight people simultaneously enter as kids playing, you'll never get the teacher, coach, or ice cream vendor.

- If you have a class of up to thirty students, have them take turns in groups of ten if you have time, and groups of fifteen if you don't. Larger numbers help stimulate imagination as more obvious "roles" are taken, and spark students to think outside the box.
- After everyone in the class has joined the environment and is playing their actions, call "Go to neutral." We encourage you to do at least two to three rounds each time.

**Example:** The initiator may decide they're in a library, and their activity is shelving books. The next person might enter and be a student studying, the next person starts sweeping the floor as a janitor, and an arriving vendor may speak to a receptionist in a normal tone, but no one is *required* to interact with one another.

*Note:* If an "honest mistake" happens—that is, a person is observed to be shelving books, and the next person thinks "Ah! We're in a bookstore!" and they enter as a barista in the store's café, encourage Yes And for participants to adapt rather than trying to fix it.

**Benefits:**

- Nurtures the ability to form and ask the question, "What does 'it' need from me?"
- Collaboration: emphasizes the importance of each individual's contribution to the whole and that the story can't be told without them.
- Helps participants understand the essential components of storytelling.
- Not only does the world not fall apart if they commit to a "smaller" role in the environment, but also the story is richer for their contribution to the story.
- Nurtures trust in one's choices and that the group will accept each contribution.
- Detailed observations: What distinguishes a universal environment? Who/what do you find in it? How can your choices be specific enough for communication to others?
- Imagination: Creating a fully realized world that needs to be communicated to others so they can also contribute to the world.

**Discussion:**

- Where were you? Try to be as specific as possible.
  - If there's a disagreement or an honest mistake about the environment (a library versus a bookstore), how could their choices have made the environment clearer?

- What role did you play in the scenario?

  - Not what characteristics they played; for example, if someone was an irate customer, and another person was a drunk customer, both were still *customers*. Who else, what else, did the environment *need*? If you had nine customers and only one cashier in a coffee shop, the group begins to understand they could have been a delivery person, health inspector, or new owner.

- Did you have an impulse to do more than what that character would normally do in that situation? Why?

  - Students discover they may not trust that they're doing "enough."

- Did you have an initial choice that someone else "took"? How easy or challenging was it to adapt to make a different choice? Did the disappointment of someone else having your idea overwhelm you, or free you to try something you might not have considered?

  - *Come Join Me* fosters collective ownership of ideas. Sometimes students feel their idea was "stolen" if someone else does it first. This can open up a healthy discussion about a person's investment in "being first," "being thought to be original," competition, and so on. So much is needed by the environment: why might they have thought that their first idea was the *only* idea available to them?

# Appendix C

## *Dinner Party*

**Focus:** Awareness, collaboration, concentration, consideration and taking care of others, focus, listening, risk taking, and trust
**How to:**

- The students are all invited to a dinner party. Have them walk about in the space and imagine they're in the foyer of a home or restaurant.
- Identify a specific line/threshold in the room that divides the foyer from where the dinner party is being held.
- Ask students to introduce themselves to one another using their real first names only. They can include a physical greeting, a wave, nod or elbow bump—whatever is safe and appropriate.
- When the introduction is over and they part, each will now take on the other person's name.

  - For example: "Hello, my name is Tom." "Nice to meet you, Tom; I'm Sergio." When that introduction is finished, Tom now has *Sergio's* name, and Sergio is now *Tom*. When they introduce themselves to the *next* person, they must use the names they received from their last encounter. Each time they meet a new person, they take on *that* person's name, and vice versa. Tom would next say, "Hello, my name is Sergio," and his new partner might say, "Hi, my name is Helen." After that introduction, Tom is now *Helen*, and Helen is *Sergio*, and so forth.

- When someone is given *their own name* back during an introduction, they are then free to go in to dinner.

- Coach students not to avoid someone who has their name to purposely prolong the game, or run toward someone that *does* have their name simply to "get out quick."
- The exercise is successfully completed when *everyone* has been given their own names back and they all get to go in to the dinner party.
- However, we invariably end up with three Allys, or two Bobs—with the *real* Ally or Bob having already gone in to dinner! It can easily take six to eight attempts (sometimes over the course of several weeks) before a group succeeds.

**Benefits:**

- The goal is that *everyone* gets to attend the dinner party; this nurtures collaboration and teamwork: "My actions affect everyone, not just *me*."
- Listening, staying focused on another person, being in the moment, not thinking ahead.
- Concentration on a task.
- Focusing on the welfare and success of the team, instead of individual success only; if the group succeeds, then each individual has succeeded.
- Meeting goals, creating strategies to meet those goals.
- Multiple repetitions of *Dinner Party* allow students to identify work habits and make adjustments to strengthen their skills each time.

*Note:* If students are struggling after several attempts, try "library" version: everyone must whisper their introductions. When given their name back, they get to "leave the library." Whispering can help with focus, attentiveness, and listening. After the group masters this version, do variations during the semester to build listening and collaboration skills: first *and* last names, or aliases.

**Discussion:**

- What skills did you need in this exercise? On reflection, what would you add to that list?
- Were you so focused on remembering what name you had that you missed the name you were given? Does that happen to you in group presentations, or in class discussions when you're waiting for "your turn"?
- Were you focused on getting everyone in to dinner, or remembering your name only? What adjustments could you make to ensure the success of the group? Can you think of a time in class where you did/didn't make an adjustment that had an impact?
- How did you feel making eye contact? What role did that play in your ability to remember the name you were given? How can you apply that observation to your retention skills overall? Do you find yourself similarly

looking at your phone or a device while communicating with others in the class, instead of making eye contact?
- Did you ever have an exchange in which you walked away, only to realize you'd forgotten to give a name to your partner? What options did that leave for your partner, and what would that mean for the group's success? Do you similarly rush yourself in schoolwork, missing important information that could support you or your classmates?
- How can eye contact and making a connection with another enhance your class skills?
- What skills did you employ to be successful with your strategies (concentration, memory and retention, empathy, awareness, etc.)? How can those skills support you in this class?
- What did you discover about your memory, focus, and retention overall? How often do you "exercise" your memory? How would you describe your process of remembering important things? Do you rely on your electronic devices to remember things for you (data, appointments, etc.), or do you use a combination of a device and your memory?
- How did you feel in the moment when the group *succeeded*? Why did it feel like such a great accomplishment? How could you apply those discoveries to our class? What adjustments could you make to be even more supportive of your peers?

# Appendix D

*Explosion Tag*

**Focus:** Awareness, commitment, playing freely, spontaneity, stamina, strategy, vulnerability
**How to:**

- All participants enter the playing area. They don't know who'll begin.
- Call out the name of a student who begins as being "it." Their goal is to tag another person; when they tag them, that person becomes "it." Whoever is not "it" has to escape from whoever is "it," like traditional tag. (However, if someone really *wants* to be "it" and you see them purposely slow down to be tagged/caught, that's OK too!)
- When a person is tagged, they must take a moment to "explode" verbally and physically, with energy. After taking a (brief) moment to explode, they then pursue someone else.

  - Examples: One person's explosion could be a loud verbal "BOOM!" accompanied by a leap in the air with arms waving wildly over their head; another might shout "Waaahooooooooo!" while tumbling in a joyous somersault; and another might squeal "Wheeeeee!" while they spin in a circle.

- The explosion should happen simultaneously with being tagged; they can take a moment to explode but should not take a moment to *think* about *how* to explode.
- After several people have had turns at being "it," or the class is huffing and puffing mightily, call "Go to neutral."

**Benefits:**

- Brings back a familiar game from childhood that allows everyone to play as adults. Everyone knows the rules; the difference is taking a beat to "explode" when tagged.
- Raises energy levels.
- Allows students to experience taking a personal moment to release and send out their energy; a physical celebration of being "it" instead of "it" being a negative.
- Brings awareness to physical stamina and breath.
- Creates greater awareness of the environment; observation.
- Sometimes students need to simply blow off steam, and *Explosion Tag* allows for wacky and fast-paced irreverence in a traditionally staid classroom.

**Discussion:**

- How would you describe your level of physical stamina?

  - If "poor," follow up and ask what they could do to improve it?

- How would you describe the relationship of your physical strength to your learning and overall well-being?
- How did it feel to explode? Were you able to allow yourself to freely explode? Did you inhibit your expression in any way? If so, why?

  - *Explosion Tag* can bring up the fear of looking silly, fear of judgment (which connects to fear of being rejected by others). Because everyone is required to do it—and all others are busy running—the exploders realize that others don't see—or care—how they explode! This can encourage students who may be reticent about participating in class to dispel their fears and contribute more.

- Did you use any strategies to avoid being it, or to try to *become* it? If so, what were they? Did they involve other people?

  - Students discover aspects of the room they may not have previously noticed and use these observations to a strategic advantage. Is there any old furniture that can create a protective barrier? Are there different levels in the room, and do they migrate to the higher level as a strategy to escape whoever is "it"?
  - Did they cluster, knowing that one person might be sacrificed, giving all others a chance to escape? What does this say about teamwork?

- How did it feel to simply run and play? What do you do in life to blow off steam or to decompress? How can this help you in your learning process?

# Appendix E

## *Freeze Tag*

**Focus:** Clarity of communication, commitment, imagination, listening, risk taking, specificity
**How to:**

- Two volunteers begin; ask them to stand a short distance in front of the class.
- One volunteer initiates a simple conflict and relationship with the other, and the partner must say Yes And to it. For example: "Sis, I need the $10 dollars I loaned you last week." It behooves Sis to say, "I don't have it, but I can get it for you soon." "Soon *when?*" "Soon." "That's not good enough; I need it now!"
- Sometimes students introduce a "situation" instead of a conflict, and the scene goes nowhere because nothing is at stake. A clear example of a conflict is to ask them to create a "Please/No" each time. "I need the $10 you owe me" (Please). "I don't have it" (No). "I need it" (Please). "I can't give you what I don't have" (No). Think of when a child is begging a parent for a toy; they may say "Please!" twenty times, but each time they realize the "Please" hasn't worked, they change their intention behind each additional "Please" (*to implore, to charm, to tease, to intimidate . . .*).
- After the conflict, characters and relationships are established, and someone from the observing group calls "Freeze!" Participants then freeze in their exact positions; the new volunteer taps one person out (that person returns to the observing group), assumes their physical position, and initiates a new conflict that's inspired by the physical position they're in. It

should *not* be a continuation of the previous scene/characters (though you can always do a variation that does allow for a continuation).
- Students can call Freeze as often as they want, but try to ensure that everyone has at least one turn. You can also require everyone to call Freeze, or you can tap students to go in. Sometimes they need a little encouragement and confidence.
- Make sure participants are initiating a conflict, and don't abdicate responsibility after calling Freeze. For example, someone calls Freeze, jumps in, and says, "What are we doing here?" That's not a conflict; that's deflecting responsibility for making a choice.
- Let a conflict and relationship be established before someone new calls Freeze.
- No invisible guns or cell phones; the conflict should be an issue between the two people, not stemming from invisible props that create avoidance, and not connection.
- After everyone has had a turn (or time is short), call for participants to go to neutral.
- *Freeze Tag* is a great opportunity to explore conflict: two opposing forces that have differing wants/goals; what's the x versus y in this scene? This is helpful when class discussions lead to different points of view in literature, sociology, or political science, or in using argument to prove a thesis in writing.
- You can do variations that may support what you're working on in your class:

  - *No Question Freeze Tag*: Same structure—two people initiate; others can call Freeze at any time once conflict is established. However, participants must only use statements; if they ask a question, they are "out" for the moment, and someone from the observing group immediately takes their place and starts a new improv. Helps students practice committing to declaring specific points of view when they speak. If they ask a question, they'll see how that deflects responsibility away from them, and moves the responsibility to the other person for the answer. They'll also experience that the story moves forward more dynamically with committed statements.
  - *Three-Word Freeze Tag*: Same structure, two people initiate, and so forth. In this variation, participants can use only three words or fewer in each exchange. Teacher creates a "warning buzzer sound" like *Jeopardy*—you can decide if they get a limited number of "buzzes" before being replaced, or they get to stay in with buzzes until someone calls Freeze. Strengthens economy and clarity of communication and increases physical expression.

## Benefits:

- Listening and being present with one another.
- Strengthens collaborative projects and class discussions if you have a group dynamic where people always feel compelled to disagree.
- Risk taking: If students get more comfortable in taking risks with low, fun stakes, they're more apt to take a risk in class. It also gives you the opportunity to say, "David, I saw how bold and imaginative you were when we did *Freeze Tag*—be bold with us now, and share your thoughts about the assignment." Once you see a student be brave and reveal their true selves to you and the class, they can't take it back!
- Finding agreement with one another: "Sis, I need that $10 I loaned you." It behooves a partner *not* to say, "Sis? I've never seen you before in my life!" That rejection stops the flow of ideas and blocks their ability to cooperate and find agreement, and for the price of a cheap laugh, one partner has abandoned the other. If someone does this—don't stop the scene and correct them; let it play out. They'll learn that after the cheap laugh line, they got nuthin.' The action stops because they've rejected the scenario, and they leave themselves with nowhere to go and nothing to build on.
- Physical awareness: Students discover that they look to one another for physical cues as well as verbal. This can encourage them to be more physically expressive and more aware of their physical expression. Think of a student who—while one of their peers is doing a presentation—does a long arm stretch with an audible yawn without covering their mouths or inhibiting the stretch.
- Taking responsibility for a choice: Students must accept and commit fully to the action and commit to a decision about what they will give their next partner.

## Discussion:

- How easy/challenging was it for you to take the initiative and call Freeze? Do you notice any correlation to what holds you back, or helps your confidence, in class?
- Did you find yourself preconceiving, or were you able to allow what the people were doing in the scene to inspire a new thought? An example of planning would be, "The minute I see someone point their finger in the air, I'll call Freeze, jump in, and shout 'Eureka! I've discovered the cure for baldness!'"

  - When students preconceive, they might wait until the ideal moment to participate in class; they will participate *only* when everything meets their specific expectations. The problem is, this ideal moment might never come up, which can lead to the student being afraid to take a risk and join in. Worse, they may be so focused on waiting for their idea/ideal moment, they won't hear or observe everyone else's contributions.

- Did you accept your partner's responses, or did you try to control their responses if they were something other than what you may have anticipated—or wanted?
- If you were holding back, why? Does that relate to how you approach assignments?
- How did it feel when your partner said Yes And to your offer? (That is, they accept that you're sisters, that money is owed, and that the stakes in the conflict are high.) What happened if a partner rejected your idea?

  - Most common reasons for rejecting a partner's offer: Trying to be funny (needing/wanting approval), desire to control, and panic they won't know what to do. Look for connections between their behavior in the exercise and their behavior in their schoolwork. Does fear block their ability to participate fully in classwork?

- What did you discover about your imagination?
- What did you learn about conflict? What created the most interesting conflicts?

  - Often, students point out that the most interesting conflicts are the simple ones: "I love you" or "It's over." Everyone gasps. The universality of these conflicts makes them compelling. Help them to connect this to class discussions: Do they ever worry that their idea is "too simple" and this holds them back? Do they focus on making something more complicated than it needs to be in order to appear "smart"? This can actually rob them of the opportunity to discover true complexities within simple ideas.

# Appendix F

## *Kitty Wants a Corner*

**Focus:** Awareness, commitment, empathy, listening, physical awareness, trust, vulnerability
**How to:**

- Participants stand in a circle with one member in the center as Kitty.
- Kitty approaches someone and asks the person to give up their spot to become Kitty and exchange places by saying, "Kitty wants a corner?" Participant responds no, and Kitty moves on to the next person, asking, "Kitty wants a corner?" No, and so on.
- During these exchanges, other members of the circle look for someone to switch places with them. They accomplish this by making eye contact, establishing *silent* agreement with each other (no gestures or head nods), and then trying to exchange places. They might run, walk, tiptoe, or whatever they think may help them succeed.
- If Kitty gets to a vacated spot before the other person does, then the person who lost their spot becomes the new Kitty and starts asking others for a corner, and so on.
- In early rounds, ask participants to always say no to Kitty. After several rounds, you can allow those in the circle to say yes to Kitty if they choose.
- Call "Go to neutral" after (a) everyone has a turn at exchanging places and/or being Kitty, or (b) their huffing and puffing inspires you to give them a break!

**Benefits:**

- Empathy and vulnerability: Eye contact is required, and a silent agreement must be made.
- Communication and connection: As empathy deepens through eye contact, agreement, and support, their investment in one another—and in the goal—deepens. These connections to each other and to common goals resonate in the classroom; it fosters respecting different points of view, support for a peer when they may be struggling, and trusting that peers—and the teacher—have everyone's best interests at heart.

  - Students experience the exhilaration of achieving something together and want more of that feeling.
  - They gain awareness of the clarity—or lack thereof—of their communication skills (nothing like *thinking* you had an agreement and realizing halfway through your run across the circle that you may have *thought* it—but you never communicated it to your partner!). This gives students insight into what they think they're communicating and what they're *actually* communicating. Also helps them get perspective on their work in class or team projects and promotes having a "clearer idea" as to how much and how hard they're actually working.

- Trust: Partners silently communicate a willingness to commit to and support their partner. If they "fail," the consequence is to become Kitty—if that's the worst part of your day, it's not so bad, is it? Students discover the difference between imagined consequences and actual ones. This leads to greater trust in themselves and in each other, which is invaluable for class discussions, group projects, and peer-review assignments.
- Physical stamina: Students by and large are more sedentary than previous generations, and a few minutes of Kitty can be a wake-up call for fitness and physical well-being.
- Physical and visual awareness: Recent studies (Feiler 2015; Stober 2012; Hietanen 2018) illustrate that with the increase of on-screen communication, there is a lessening of abilities to read social cues, including body language and facial expressions. Strengthening these skills supports clarity of communication in class and enhances students' ability to read social cues *and* your ability to read theirs.
- Risk taking: It's risky to look into someone else's eyes and make an agreement without words, and risky to rely on another and trust them to honor their commitment to you.
- Commitment and confidence: Kitty encourages following through on commitments, and taking risks via commitment builds confidence.

**Discussion:**

*Appendix F*

- What communication skills did you employ? Did you struggle with eye contact? If so, why? Did you discover skills that you could bring to your classwork?
- What did the "silent agreement" mean to you? Were you able to communicate with less than what you thought you'd need? How could that relate to communications in class?
- Did you find yourselves "rooting" for Kitty or the Exchangers as a move was being made? Why? How does empathy play a role?
- What did you discover about the perceived "consequences" of being Kitty?

  - Many students discover that the consequence—becoming Kitty—is actually *fun*; the perceived "failure" doesn't stop the exercise. For others, it can bring up feelings of "being picked last" for teams, or fears of rejection. No one is ever Kitty for the entire time—see bullet below.

- When you were Kitty, did you anticipate "failure"? During the "yes" round, did you ever miss someone's yes because you were worried you would never find "a corner"? How can anticipating rejection block us from realizing our full potential?
- How sensitive did you all become to one another's energy? Did you notice that you could "sense" someone about to move before they did, that you felt their energy "rise"?
- How did you feel if you committed to, and then reneged, on your agreement with your partner, and they became the new Kitty? Has someone ever made a commitment to you in a group project in class, and then not come through? Why did people block or avoid their partners in Kitty? Fear? Worry that a partner wouldn't be there for you? How can understanding these reasons help your understanding of one another in classwork?

# Appendix G

## *Observe 6*

**Focus:** Awareness, empathy, focus, memory, observation, retention, vulnerability
**How to:**

- Students work with a partner; we suggest calling out numbers 1–2–3–4, and pairing up according to number, so students don't work with a friend whom they're very familiar with.
- Once partnered, determine one partner to be A, the other B.
- Ask them to silently observe one another, noting details (hair, clothing, etc.).
- After a short period of observation, ask partners to turn their backs to one another.
- With backs turned, call out for As to go first. They are now to change six aspects of their appearance. Switch a piece of jewelry to another wrist or finger, put their hair up if it's down, remove a shoe or belt, tuck a pantleg into a sock . . .
- After As have changed six things about their appearance, call "go!" Partners turn to each other. Bs must identify the six changes. After a brief period, ask for a show of hands as to who is still in the guessing phase.
- When B has successfully guessed the six changes, or when time is up, partners turn their backs to each other again and B changes six things about their appearance. Repeat steps.
- You can begin with changing only three aspects of appearance and build up to six. If students do well, you can continue to challenge them by making it seven, eight, or nine changes.

- If the class knows each other well, have them change partners after each round so A doesn't have the advantage of having observed B longer during the guessing phase.
- Advise students that the change must be tangible in appearance (not a facial expression) and in full view. That is, if you switch a penny from your left pocket to your right pocket, it doesn't count!

**Benefits:**

- Strengthens observation skills and attention to detail.
- Improves memory and retention. What if you were called upon to describe the person who's sitting next to you?
- Develops empathy. It's intimate to silently look at another person as you try to take in details about them. It's also vulnerable to be looked at that closely, with such intention.
- Strengthens communication skills.
- Concentration and focus: In having a specific task focused solely on another person, students learn to shut out distractions and focus on the task at hand.

**Discussion:**

- How did you feel looking so intently at your partner, and being looked *at* so intently?
- What did you notice about the strength of your skills of observation? (Try to avoid words like "good" or "bad.") If you didn't guess all changes, did you get stronger as you repeated the exercise? How could you strengthen your observation and memory skills in life?
- What can you adjust in the future to successfully guess the changes? How could you relate this to adjustments you can make to how you approach classwork?
- Did you notice a pattern in your observations? For example, you remembered every detail about clothing and jewelry, but not changes in hair. Is there any correlation to things you remember from class discussions or reading assignments? Do you tend to remember and retain things you enjoy and gloss over those that don't interest you as much? What could you adjust so that you retain more than just what you personally "like"?
- Did you struggle to pay attention? What stole your focus? Does this happen in class?
- Was it easy or challenging to come up with six changes to your appearance? Were you doubting your choices? How does this relate to your confidence about making decisions?

- How could you do this exercise in your daily life to strengthen memory and retention? Choose a room in your house; describe it in detail, including colors and textures of items.

# Appendix H

## *One-Word-at-a-Time Storytelling*

**Focus:** Collaboration, focus, listening, respecting the choices of others, team building
**How to:**

- Students stand in a circle.
- One student starts the story with one word, and each person in turn adds another word to the story. "Once—upon—a—time—there—was—a—fox."
- The story continues until you decide to bring it to a close, or the ensemble collectively agrees it's finished.
- Encourage the students to tell a complete, cohesive story, rather than a random collection of sentences about unrelated people or topics.
- After they try it a few times, aim to tell the story with the same rate and inflection as if one person were telling it: no pauses between words, no dismissive offering of a word by making it a question, and no sounds or inflections to suggest judgment of another student's offer.
- Often, especially in the early attempts, the story will fall apart. A student will draw a blank or offer a word that doesn't make grammatical or logical sense. Encourage students to continue, to trust their instincts and make the story work for them, even if it isn't initially cohesive. The students will improve as they continue this exercise, and discussions afterward about what happened can greatly assist them in making adjustments going forward.

# ALTERNATIVE: STORYTELLING CHORUS

**How to:**

- Similar to *One-Word-at-a-Time Storytelling*, but line the students up in one to three rows facing you, like a choir.
- Instead of going in an order one word at a time, gesture (avoid pointing) at one of the students, who then begins to tell a story. An open-palm gesture works really well, as if inviting them to join you on the dance floor.
- The student continues the story until you gesture to stop. The student immediately stops, even if in the middle of a word or sentence.
- Gesture to another student at random. That student picks up the story right where it left off, midword or midsentence, and continues until you gesture to stop. Gesture to another student at random, and so on.
- The story continues until you feel it has successfully ended, or when the ensemble collectively agrees to end it.

**Benefits:**

- Collaboration skills: Regardless of the offered word, story element, or plot twist, the students are taking what they're given and working together to tell the story.
- Listening: Students must listen to not just the student who contributes a word before them but also to all the students and the story as a whole. They won't have time to plan and come up with "the perfect" contribution. They can only listen and play.
- Yes And: Students need to build on the choices of their partners and honor those choices by saying yes to them, whether it's a story element they would have chosen or not. The word or phrase they then add is the "and."
- Judgment and spontaneity: Students don't have time to harshly judge their contribution to the story, or the contributions of others.
- Focus and concentration: It can be challenging for students to maintain their composure if the story falters, but they must continue to build upon one another's choices.

**Discussion:**

- Did you go with your first impulse when it was your turn, or did you pause and try to find the "right" answer? How can you make sure you always contribute to building—or ending—the story? Reflect on what being "right" and being "wrong" means to you in life, and how that affects your classwork.

- Were there any unexpected story elements? When it was your turn, was your word hard to come up with? Did you persevere and trust your partners to continue the story?
- If the story got confusing, how did you handle it? Did you try to steer it in another direction, rely on your partners to do so, or trust you'd all build it together? How can you trust your classmates to build upon something similar in the classroom?
- When did you lose concentration? What can you do to keep your focus? How can you apply similar concentration techniques in the classroom? In studying?
- Did you successfully avoid judging your partners' choices, or not? What did you lose by spending time judging, and how can you accept every offer given to you?
- What did this game reveal about your desire to control? What could it mean when we try to control someone's choices? How does that lack of trust inhibit your progress?

# Appendix I

## *Simultaneous Clap*

**Focus:** Collaboration, concentration, empathy, focus, honesty, listening, team building

**How to:**

- Students stand in a circle and designate one person to begin: person A.
- Person A turns to whoever is on their left side: person B. The goal is for those two people to clap their hands simultaneously.
- A and B attempt to clap their hands simultaneously, without any verbal discussion of how to do it. A and B make as many attempts as needed; when they achieve a simultaneous clap, B then turns to the person on their left: person C.
- B and C attempt to clap their hands simultaneously, and so on. Once the simultaneous clap is achieved, C then turns to the person on their left, and the process continues.
- The goal is to try to have one full round in the circle with each set of partners only needing one clap to achieve synchronicity.
- Honesty is important; be sure to stop any duo who attempts to "move along" in the circle if they haven't yet achieved synchronicity in their claps together.
- We've noticed that once students achieve the synchronicity as a group, the circular passing of the claps picks up speed and finds a specific rhythm. Once that collective rhythm is established, the synchronicity happens with more frequency.

**Benefits:**

- Empathy: The eye contact in this exercise can be intense, and the synchronicity depends upon the partners' success in "reading" one another. This can only happen if they're taking each other in and actively putting themselves in each other's shoes.
- Observation: The nonverbal communication emphasizes the need for partners to fully communicate with one another; eye contact and body language play a big role.
- Collaboration: Partners are trying to achieve something together, and ultimately for the entire group. This fosters deeper connections in class and makes it harder to "dismiss" someone who learns at a different pace or has a different point of view.
- Honesty: Partners need to achieve the simultaneous clap and agree on the moment when that's achieved before the clap moves further in the circle.
- Concentration: Partners need to figure out why they're *out* of sync when working toward synchronicity and find a solution and agreement without discussing it verbally.

**Discussion:**

- What did you notice as you worked out how to clap simultaneously? How did you and your partner communicate? In class, how aware are you of one another's body language?
- How did you feel when you achieved the synchronicity with your partner? How can achieving that kind of agreement with a partner enhance your work together in class?
- What did you notice about your partners? How would you describe the energy itself and any adjustments or tactics you observed partners making to achieve synchronicity?
- What happened when partners achieved synchronicity in one attempt? How did it feel when that was passed through the circle?
- If it took you several attempts to achieve synchronicity, what might that tell you about how you communicate? What adjustments could you make?
- When trying to achieve the simultaneous clap, what helped you stay with your partner and have faith you could do it? Did anything make you want to give up, on yourself or your partner? If so, what was within your power to do to support your success?
- How did achieving synchronicity with your partner affect the success of the task?

# Appendix J

## *Three-Headed Alien*

**Focus:** Collaborative learning, listening, relief of stress, taking care of your partner, Yes And
**How to:**

- Choose three students to be the *Three-Headed Alien*; they can either stand side by side, or sit in three chairs closely set to one another.
- Choose to be the interviewer yourself, or select one of your more confident students to interview the alien.
- The interviewer introduces the alien to the class and presents the alien as an expert in all subjects.
- The interviewer asks a question, and then each person within the three-headed alien must answer one word at a time; that is, each head is allowed to say only a single word in each turn, to cumulatively build a response to the question. One of the three heads must decide or sense when the response is "complete."
- Responses may be a single word, a single sentence, or multiple sentences. After a series of questions are answered by the alien, stop the exercise and begin a new round with a new three-headed alien and interviewer.
- With each new question, either you can start with whoever is the first head or each new answer can begin with whatever head you left off at. After students familiarize themselves with the exercise, the interviewer can open it up and take questions from the "audience."

## Benefits:

- Collaboration skills: Each response should make sense in relation to the question.
- Listening: Each head needs to listen carefully to what has come before. In this way, they remain present, attentive, and in the moment.
- Yes And: Each head needs to build upon the choices of their partners and honor those choices by saying yes to them, whether it's something they would have chosen or not.
- Judgment and spontaneity: Each student doesn't have time to harshly judge any contribution to the response.
- Focus and concentration: As you can imagine, things can get fairly silly, and it can be a challenge for the three heads to maintain their composure.

## Discussion:

- Did you commit to your first impulse when it was your turn, or did you pause and try to find the "right" answer? What can you do to make sure you always have something to say that contributes to building—or ending—answers in the classroom?
- Were there any questions you didn't expect? How did you handle it? How might this approach benefit you during class discussions?
- When did you lose concentration? Was there ever a moment when you didn't know how to add the next word? What can you do to keep your focus?
- Did you accept the others' contributions, or did you silently wish they'd chosen a different word? What did you lose by spending time in judgment, and what can you do to avoid it and accept everything handed to you?
- What helped you "get in sync" with your partners? Making eye contact? How did it feel when you achieved synchronicity, and how can you apply that to class?

# Appendix K

## Walk and Rename Objects (Keith Johnstone)

**Focus:** Commitment to choices, relationship to environment, focus, imagination, observation
**How to:**

- Have the class walk (silently) in the room; encourage them to take up as much space as possible. Notice their body language. Who's looking at the floor? Who seems to doubt that they know *how* to walk (shuffling, stopping frequently)? Who seems bored or nervous? Whose arms are crossed, and whose arms are swinging playfully?
- Observe how they fill they room with their energy, and ask them to try to imagine where their personal center of energy might be located. In their heart? Belly? Head?
- Ask them to point to any object in the room, and rename it—out loud. They can call it anything except what that object *literally* is; for example, a chair is a flower, or a backpack is a sofa. They can point to light switches and fixtures, and so on.
- Side-coach them to rename as many objects as possible. They can return to the same object but create a different name for it.
- After a while, have them pause from verbal renaming and continue to walk in the room. Does the room seem smaller or larger? Have a lower or higher ceiling?
- Begin the renaming process again; they can create new names for objects they've already "christened."
- Go to neutral. Take one full breath, and relax the body.

- This is a game they can do on their own (silently), on their walk to and from school, or while crossing campus.

**Benefits:**

- Students get away from their desks and get physically energized.
- Awareness and ownership of one's physical environment: What surrounds them? What are the things they walk past every day? How can that awareness present opportunities for their learning?

  - It also strengthens their relationship to the room itself: if something feels like "home," they're likely to feel more comfortable and more confident.

- Observation skills: Everything that surrounds them is a playful opportunity. That can stimulate their imaginations, while considering that everything they encounter throughout their day may be meaningful, inspiring, or interesting. This can help students become more observant in class discussions, homework assignments, reading, and test taking.
- Strengthens focus and memory skills: Because of the act of giving each item its own original name, *Walk and Rename Objects* empowers students to take ownership of all they encounter. If they notice and remember more in their life, it strengthens their ability to listen to lectures, read chapters, study for tests, and further engage in classroom activities.
- Imagination and commitment to imaginative choices: Helps students who worry about being wrong or lack confidence. Encourages imagination, play, and the limitless resources that each student has. The more names they create, the more they realize how much they have to contribute.
- Confidence: The act of "renaming" an item allows students a safe structure to explore that there is no right or wrong. This builds confidence to take risks in class. Once they've experienced "what's the worst that could happen if I call this desk an orangutan?" then taking a chance by raising their hand gets a little easier.

**Discussion:**

- What did you notice about the environment when the exercise was over? Did you notice more of your surroundings?

  - Often a student says, "I've been in this room a hundred times, but I've never noticed that blue chair/dent in the door." This exercise opens up discussions about observation, awareness, and how lacking these can lead to missed opportunities. It inspires students to observe familiar places in their life to see what else they may have overlooked.

- How comfortable were you in taking ownership of your relationship to "new" objects and to the space? If you struggled, does that correlate to your personal confidence in taking ownership of the subject material or of your learning in class?
- How did you feel about having the power to rename an object?
- Did you begin to see the object differently once you renamed it? Did your imagination make it seem larger, smaller, or have a different value (e.g., if a chalk eraser became a gold ingot, or a desk became your grandmother's walnut dining table)?
- How does this newfound awareness relate to your awareness outside of the classroom?

  - Give students a fun quiz: Ask about landmarks on campus that they walk past every day, or the color of their bedroom at home. Have them close their eyes and describe what you or the person on their right or left is wearing? How can strengthening observation skills support learning skills overall?

- Did you struggle to let go of what the object literally was and block your imaginative impulses, or did you feel you could have come up with a hundred names for each item? What might that tell you about *how* you learn or think?

# Appendix L

## *What Are You Doing?*

**Focus:** Awareness, clarity of communication, commitment, imagination, listening, stamina
**How to:** Two people face one another: person A and person B. Other participants form single-file lines behind each of them (same amount of people behind each person if possible).

- Person A asks person B, "What are you doing?"
- B responds by stating a simple physical activity: "I'm brushing my teeth."
- A immediately starts to brush their teeth, while B runs to the back of their line.
- The person who was standing behind person B steps up (person C) and asks A, "What are you doing?"
- Person A, *while continuing to do the action they were given* (brushing their teeth), states a new action to person C: "I'm bouncing a basketball." Then A runs to the back of their line.
- Person C immediately starts to bounce a basketball, while the person standing behind A (person D) steps up to ask C, "What are you doing?"
- Person C, while *continuing to bounce the basketball*, gives a new physical action to D and then runs to the back of their own line, and so on.
- Do the exercise long enough so that everyone has many turns at this.
- If someone gives an action that the other person doesn't understand, ask them to commit to what they *imagine* it to be. We once had a student who, in her panic, gave the action in her native language—we don't remember her language or the phrase, but it was something like "I'm veshnoofing ze veshnoofdicator." Her partner paused for a split second and then commit-

ted to an action that was inspired by what she imagined veshnoofing ze veshnoofdicator would be!
- If they plan, they experience the feeling of having "rejected" their partner's offer and sense their lack of trust. When they don't plan, they experience "what's the worst that can happen?" and discover that "the well is never dry"—because the water in that metaphorical well is replenished by their collaborators every moment.

**Benefits:**

- Confidence building: There's no right or wrong answer.
- Listening and observation: Students allow themselves to be inspired by the previous person's choice, which encourages them to listen and observe more closely in class.
- Committing to first choices and taking risks.
- Listening to, and acting on, impulsive choices.

  - Discourage students from being hard on themselves if they "repeat" an action ("I'm terrible at this; I said "eating a taco" three times!"). They're stretching the impulse muscle, and that's more important than not repeating something.

- Students discover that *everything* that comes before their "turn" is part of their inspiration. Their "turn" is only one part of the larger story, and when they allow themselves to take in everything that comes before their turn, their responses are connected. In class discussions, if a student listens to everyone's contribution, they're more likely to have an idea that's built upon what's just been shared.

**Discussion:**

- How did you feel when it was your turn? Did you plan, or were you open to your impulses?
- If you planned, why? What might you have missed by focusing on your planned choice while others were actively doing their choices?
- If you were open in the moment, how did it feel when your choice "came to you"? How might this relate to your classwork?
- Were you able to commit fully to your choices? If so, what helped you to commit? If not, what got in your way? Are you ever tentative in your responses in class?
- What did you learn about your listening and observation skills? If something was getting in your way, what was it? Does that "thing" also get in

your way in class discussions, group work, or test taking? What can you do about the thing that blocks you?

# Appendix M

## *Zing*

**Focus:** Awareness, empathy, ensemble and team building, group connection, listening
**How to:**

- The goal is for everyone to send and receive Zing, and to consistently pass the energy to one another in the circle.
- The class forms a circle: Zing is an invisible ball of energy that each member sends to another with a specific arm gesture (we prefer the arm elongated with the hand open, palm sideways but aimed in the direction of the other person; this way we're not "pointing a finger"—which can create anxiety—and the direction of the offer is clear and open). Students make eye contact while doing the gesture and saying the word "Zing" simultaneously. Eye contact is important; it can and should be brief.
- As soon as a person receives Zing, they send it to someone else while making eye contact, with a physical arm gesture, and Zing is passed randomly around the circle.
- At some point when Zing comes back to the teacher (yes, you can participate too!) and you feel you've accomplished why you wanted to do Zing, call, "And one–two–three to the middle . . . Zing!" while physically doing a gesture to the center and everyone saying (and gesturing) the final Zing to the center together.
- Students should focus on sending Zing impulsively to another person, and not stop to think about "who needs Zing." Nor should they get involved in a competition (two students sending Zing fiercely back and forth to one another, excluding the group).

- Never, ever allow "Zing elimination." *Zing* is very similar to another theater (and pub!) game called Zip Zap Zop, which is often done with elimination. If someone drops the Zing or loses focus, simply guide them to pick it back up again. The only consequence is to get to try it again.
- It's immediately noticeable when someone "drops" Zing or loses focus because of the physical/vocal aspects. Sometimes it's dropped because of the intensity that builds.
- Encourage students to pick up the tempo if they're lagging—are they sending/receiving Zing as quickly as they can? It's not about speed but about whether they're "in the flow."
- You have some options with *Zing*:

    - You can begin with the impulsive/random version, and then at some point call, "side to side." Zing can then only be sent to one's immediate left or right—however, they can change directions if they feel the impulse to do so. They shouldn't change directions just because they want to "control" Zing, or to get into a competition with a friend.
    - During Side-to-Side *Zing*, the guide can call "One Direction"; this means whatever direction Zing is flowing in at that time, it continues in that direction only. Zing then picks up speed—be mindful that participants aren't "getting ahead" but fully receiving Zing before sending it to the next partner.
    - After students have done *Zing* a few times, introduce Freak Out version. During the random passing of Zing, someone calls "Freak Out!"; everyone then waves their arms, or does wild gestures, breaks up the circle, and runs around the room for a moment or two; then the circle needs to reconstitute. Zing can't begin again until the circle has reformed with all participants; then someone takes the initiative to begin Zing again. This continues until the leader decides to change versions, or do one–two–three to the middle final Zing.

**Benefits:**

- Being present and attentive: The exercise moves quickly; a student can't afford to be disconnected or unfocused.
- Empathy: The eye contact and intentional passing of energy from one to the other allows students to connect and to literally see how their partner is feeling.
- Being open and receptive; allowing one's self to be vulnerable
- The ability to be open to and affected by others: *Zing* blossoms when a group allows themselves to be affected by what another person gives them. If someone with low energy insists on rejecting an energetic offer, it becomes clear that they were closed off.

*Appendix M* 163

- Strengthening impulsive responses: The speed of the exercise doesn't allow for doubt, which encourages participants to be attuned to first impulses and ideas.
- Being energized, pure and simple: *Zing* gets a person going. It's simple to do, fun to master, and allows for playful connection; individuals discover that their energy and mood can be changed, and the group's collective energy evolves and grows too.

**Discussion:**

- What did you notice about your energy at the beginning of the exercise, and at the end? If it changed, what was responsible for the change? What happens when you arrive to class and feel low energy, or you're in a mindset that isn't conducive to learning? What could you change about your state of mind, and how could the group facilitate that?
- Are you stopping to think about what to do or who you *should* send Zing to, or are you simply doing it? What makes you judge your choices instead of trying them to see if they'll work? What role does self-judgment play in your classwork?
- How did it feel to make eye contact throughout the exercise? What difference did it make if you didn't make eye contact?

  - Students may say eye contact "feels weird"; it's a critical component of learning and nurturing empathy. Empathy is at the core of what binds a society together; have a conversation about the role of empathy and the difference it can make in your class. It plays a role in group projects, student preparation ("If I let myself down, I let the class down"), and mutual respect of one another.

    - It also contributes mightily to the "cell phone arguments" you may have with a student: "I was listening; I was just looking at my phone." If this comes up, ask them why they feel more comfortable looking at a screen instead of another person's face.

- How did you feel about the Zing itself? Was there a sense of personal or group responsibility? How does that connect to the group's responsibility for learning in class?
- What helped you to trust your partners?
- When trust was created, what did that affect?

  - If students say, "Once I trusted that everyone was committed to giving one another Zing, there was less pressure if someone made a mistake," ask, "So what could we do in class to create a supportive environment in which everyone feels encouraged to participate, whether their answer is spot on or not?"

# Appendix N

## *Physical Exercise: Home Rehearsal for Teachers*

**Focus:** Health, physical strength and flexibility, physical expressiveness, stamina
**How to:**

**First Try:**

- Set aside at least one hour; wear loose clothing that you're comfortable moving in. You'll need a timer and a room with enough space to move in.
- Reread your syllabus for the semester. Set a timer for sixty seconds. Imagine someone that you know and trust is in the room with you, someone unfamiliar with your subject and your class. Now imagine that you need to communicate the Story of This Syllabus to your friend, without words, using your physical movement only, in sixty seconds—start the timer, and go! There's no right or wrong; this will simply give you useful information about how you work, and what you may want to keep or adjust.

**Benefits:**

- Physical awareness; personal connection to body and personal expression.
- Clarity and specificity of physical communication.
- Builds empathy: The more connected and confident you are about the content, the more you'll understand the journey the students need to take with the material.
- Encourages creativity and imagination in reviewing any subject.
- Builds confidence through practice/rehearsal.

- Exercises abstract thinking and expression.

**Reflection Questions after First Round:**

- What was your first impulse? To be literal and start with the very first thing on the syllabus, or to find a singular movement or gesture to capture the overall essence?
- Did you repeat a certain gesture? If so, is it a gesture that you habitually do outside of your work, or only when you teach?
- Did you communicate the subject matter, the goal of the class itself, or both?
- What aspects of the story did you feel were clearly communicated?
- What did you omit? Would your listener understand the material without it?
- How did you feel when the timer stopped?

**Second Try:**

- Reread the syllabus, and take a few moments to reflect after this second read. Reset the timer for sixty seconds, and do the exercise again. If you want to change your imaginary friend, go ahead.

**Reflection Questions after Second Round:**

- What did you notice this time? Was there any movement or gesture that carried over from the first time?
- Did your movement choices become more abstract, or more realistic? For example, when trying to express an atom, its power, and makeup, were you literally drawing elliptical lines in the air to form the image? Or did you scrunch your body into the tiniest ball possible, and then leap into the air with arms and legs wide to express explosion?
- When describing the structure of an English class essay, did you place the introduction higher in the air? The conclusion lower toward the ground?
- When approaching a difficult aspect of a course—for example, graphing algebraic equations—did you wave your hands in the air like a presto-change-o magic trick? Did you swipe it aside in a dismissive gesture of "we'll get to this later"? What does this tell you about your relationship to the content?
- When describing an arts or music class, did you find surprisingly clear gestures that represented difficult concepts? Interlacing fingertips for abstract art? Palms out for still life? A fist for a whole note or a rest?

Try the exercise a third time, and a fourth, especially if you find this challenging. If the exercise inspires you to make significant changes to your syllabus, do the exercise again from the beginning once your revisions are complete. Jot down notes between each round, and include any responses your imagined "friend" might say about your sixty-second physical presentation.

You can also do this exercise for lesson plans, invited lectures, or faculty meetings.

# Appendix O

## *Laban Movement Analysis*

In chapter 4, we outlined how you could learn and apply some broader aspects of the Laban Movement Analysis. The first part of the exploration focused on the four categories of movement: (1) space: direct/indirect, (2) weight: strong/light, (3) time: quick/sustained, and (4) flow: bound/free. Space, time, and weight have additional movement adjectives for greater specificity. Watch your footage again, and have this list of "action efforts" nearby. They are as follows:

- Float (indirect, sustained, light)
- Dab (direct, quick, light)
- Punch (direct, quick, heavy)
- Press (direct, sustained, heavy)
- Slash (indirect, quick, heavy)
- Wring (indirect, sustained, heavy)
- Glide (direct, sustained, light)
- Flick (indirect, quick, light)

What specific physical actions can you add to your description? Would you describe your movement or gestures as a flick, or a punch in the air? Look at the list again; what adjectives come to mind in describing the energy associated with those descriptors? Tentative, aggressive, ethereal, or dynamic? Is your movement serving your lesson plan, and would you like to change anything?

Try not to overanalyze or focus on the minutiae of your movements, or whether you personally "look good." Explore the types of movement that most draw you to the person talking on camera (you). Sustained and press? Direct and glide? Which gestures made you feel you weren't invited into the story? Direct and punch? Choose two movements to adjust, do the exercise again, and observe those changes.

After you've chosen movements that support your intention, go through your lesson plan or lecture and score it; assign movement descriptors. Practice it with those physical actions/descriptors. If they don't feel natural, try different ones that feel more personal to you and your goals. You won't need to think about what to do with your hands; you'll feel the difference in how connected you feel to your intention and in how confident you feel in your body.

# Appendix P

## *Vocal Warm Up*

Your voice is completely reliant on the strength and flexibility of your breath and physical body. One of the greatest causes of vocal struggles is tension and stress, so it's important to include relaxation exercises for your face, tongue, jaw, neck, and so forth. Try not to be tempted to skip them to get to the tongue twisters!

**Exercise 1:** Neck rolls. Stand with your feet about shoulder-width apart; imagine an invisible string going up through your spine, through the top of your head. The string isn't pulling you off your toes; it's gently pulling the top of your head upward, to create supportive alignment in your spine, neck, and head. Now imagine the string is released a bit; your chin gently drops to your chest—be sure your neck and shoulders don't collapse. Slowly roll your head to the right, so that your right ear is over your right shoulder. Gently roll your head to the left until your left ear is over your left shoulder.

Allow your neck to follow its natural arc; don't robotically "place" your left ear over left shoulder, and so forth. On slow counts of four, roll your head to the right again, and then slowly to the left. Allow the natural weight of your head to guide you and your mouth to fall open as your head rolls right and left (note if you're clenching your jaw). Try not to hyper-extend, and don't roll your head backward as this could compress your vertebrae and damage your neck.

**Exercise 2:** Lion/Mouse. This exercise stretches and enlivens your facial muscles. Start with Lion Face: allow your face to be as big as possible and yes, to look like a lion! Open your mouth wide, stick your tongue out, allow the muscles in your forehead to raise, release breath, and make a sound. Hold the face for a count of three. Quickly change to Mouse Face: scrunch your facial muscles as tiny as they can go; purse your lips, squinch your eyes, and release what feels like a "tiny mouse" sound. Hold for a count of three.

Now, go back to Lion Face—see if your mouth can open wider. Hold for three counts, go back to Mouse Face, and so on. After four to five sets of Lion/Mouse, allow your facial muscles to relax. If you know how to flap your lips like a horse, this would be a good time to add to the menagerie.

If you're feeling shy at first about doing Lion/Mouse, give yourself a simple face massage. Gently, using two to three fingers, start with your forehead, massaging both sides in small, slow rotating circles. Be sure to get the area around your eyes (you'd be surprised how much tension we hold in our eyebrows and foreheads). Move down to the area below the eyes and your temples. Experiment with the amount of pressure you apply to each area; this will tell you where you may be holding tension. When you get to your jaw, spend a little extra time massaging the area of the hinge and lower jaw.

**Exercise 3:** Tongue stretch. Your tongue is a major muscle in the support of this work, and it can become stronger and more flexible with exercise. There are multiple online videos that you can reference (and yes, these are the exercises where you can look and feel pretty silly—embrace it!), but here are a few simple steps to start (use a mirror to help guide you).

- Stretch your tongue out as far as it can go, hold, and retract. Do this five times.
- Stretch your tongue out, and *try* to touch the tip of your nose. Don't worry if you don't achieve that; simply try the physical action. Now, extend your tongue and try to touch your chin. Try this sequence five times, and try to hold the tongue in place a bit longer each time.
- With your mouth closed, press the tip of your tongue against the roof of your mouth. Slowly, curl your tongue and press it against the roof; after hitting the soft palate, return to original position and repeat.
- Place the tip of your tongue against the back of your teeth, and with mouth open, arch the middle of your tongue through the opening, hold, and return. This stretch often reveals whether you tend to hold tension in your tongue or not.

**Exercise 4:** Stretch muscles between the ribs and diaphragm (these are also great for relaxation). Stand with feet shoulder-width apart, raise your left arm, and stretch to your right side. Be sure your knees are slightly bent/soft and not "locked." This gently stretches your intercostals; you can also bring your right arm across your body, and gently pat your left side to help with release. Return to neutral; now raise your right arm, stretch to the left, and so forth. Notice your breath, especially in your lower ribs. Repeat this sequence three to four times; try to extend the "hold" each time.

Next, imagine you're stretching "forward and back." Clasp your hands behind your back, and gently raise them an inch or two. You should feel the stretch in your chest, opening it further (it also feels good after sitting at your desk for far too long).

After holding for a few beats, release your arms, and now bring them around to give yourself a great hug, with shoulders rounded. You should feel this stretch in the muscles of your upper back. If you like, you can deepen this by holding the hug and gently rolling down one vertebrae at a time until you're still hugging but gently hanging from your waist. Hold for several beats, continue to notice your breath, and gently roll back up one vertebrae at a time.

**Exercise 5:** Breath. Breath literally creates the voice and gives it life. Are you able to fill a sentence with breath from start to finish, or do you run out of air and gasp, or "snatch" at the air for a quick inhale mid thought? Are you able to fill the words themselves, vowels bordered with crisp consonants? Are you exhausted after a twenty- to thirty-minute lecture? Have students ever asked you to speak up? You may simply not be getting enough oxygen.

One of the simplest ways to increase breath capacity is through timed inhalations and exhalations. Stand, feet shoulder-width apart; inhale on a count of four, hold on a count of four, and exhale on a count of four. Try several sets of the lower number. Gradually, increase that count by one each time. Inhale for five counts, hold for five counts, and exhale for five counts. If you start to feel light-headed, take a short break and breathe "normally." Take note of how you breathe: Shallow breaths? Deep breaths? Do you breathe from the diaphragm, or from the throat?

**Exercise 6:** Speech. Clarity and specificity with sound is one of your greatest tools to combine with the muscularity of a strong voice. Start with simple tongue twisters, even if you haven't done one since second grade. They'll help you with pronunciation and clarity, and they strengthen the muscles of your tongue, lips, and mouth—think of it like mouth weight-lifting. Overenunciate while repeating these, and notice any sounds that are challenging for you. We all remember "Peter Piper picked a peck of pickled peppers," but here are a few more:

- Unique New York.
- The big black bug bit the big black bear.
- She sells seashells by the seashore.
- The sixth sick sheikh's sixth sheep's sick.
- Fuzzy Wuzzy was a bear. Fuzzy Wuzzy had no hair. Fuzzy Wuzzy wasn't fuzzy, was he?

**Exercise 7:** For quality of tone/breath. Many of us have felt the strain after teaching back-to-back (to back) classes, or the rasp that can come after a two-hour lecture, or we've run out of breath in the middle of describing a math problem or analyzing a passage from a novel. Strengthening and expanding your vocal ability is going to give you a power, resonance, and flexibility with your voice that has the potential to make a profound difference.

After identifying key points in your lesson plan, or the climax of the story, your vocal strength and muscularity will help drive those points home to your students. That may mean not "more volume" (though it could) but that you'd have the facility to vocally create a rise and fall with the points you're making, more readily bring inflection to operative words, and bring your own emotion and passion for the topic into your expression.

Read aloud this single sentence from Dr. Carleton Jones's book *Temples of Stone: Exploring the Megalithic Tombs of Ireland*: "Mountains, like rivers, are large distinctive features in the landscape and throughout the world mountains are also frequently regarded as sacred sites."

1. Read this out loud, flatly, with no difference in vocal inflection, and not enough available breath to say the sentence with breath through to the end.
2. Now, take a full breath before reading aloud. Have an image for each word: What does the word "mountain" feel like when you say it, if you were trying to express it to someone who has never seen a mountain before? How do *you* feel when you see a beautiful mountain for the first time? Give a different value to how you say "river"; you're making a comparison, but they're two distinctly different landscape features. What's the first point? Mountains are important and they're *distinctive* in the landscape, not only in one region but throughout the entire *world*. That's a big and expansive idea to communicate, so you can expand your voice while you tell this part of the story. Why should we care about how distinctive mountains are? So many cultures from around the world have considered mountains to be *sacred sites*. That so many different people from varied time periods often came to similar conclusions is an exciting mystery to be explored, and that's the second main point. As you build the story contained in this single sentence, you can convey excitement, a sense of wonder, and a desire to want to find out more, all in how you vocally deliver it. Thus: "Mountains, like *rivers*, are large *distinctive* features in the landscape and throughout the *world* mountains are also *frequently* regarded as *sacred sites*."

Breaking down language and intention in this way can expand your already considerable flexibility and vocal power for a lesson, and for a semester. Even trying a few sentences will start the ball—and your imagination—

rolling, and you'll intuitively find more depth as you continue. It's well worth the investment of making a lion and a mouse face.

# Appendix Q

## *The Uta Hagen Nine Questions*

The following nine questions comprise Uta Hagen's primary method of character analysis for an actor, and the relationship of their character to the world of the play.

1. Who am I? (identity)
2. What time is it? (the present moment of time, the season of the year, as well as the moment of time in society at large)
3. Where am I? (your location at this moment and your relationship to it; the elements in this environment)
4. What surrounds me? (objects, people, animals, plants, anything in your environment)
5. What are the given circumstances? (all that has happened to bring you to this present moment, and all the conditions that surround you now [environment, personal, societal] that influence your actions)
6. What is my relationship? (to other characters/people, objects, events, environment, time)
7. What do I want? (objective, want, need)
8. What's in my way? (obstacles/blocks that you face)
9. What do I do to get what I want? (the physical or verbal actions you take in pursuit of achieving your objective)

# Appendix R

*Exercises for Ice Breakers, Getting Acquainted*

- *Dinner Party*
- *Kitty Wants a Corner*
- *Observe 6*
- *Simultaneous Clap*
- *What Are You Doing?*
- *Zing*

# Appendix S

*Exercises to Strengthen Collaborative Skills*

- *Blind Offers*
- *Come Join Me*
- *Count to 20*
- *Dinner Party*
- *One-Word-at-a-Time Storytelling*
- *Three-Headed Alien*

# Appendix T

*Exercises to Develop Imagination and Empowerment*

- *Come Join Me*
- *Freeze Tag*
- *Slow-Motion Tag*
- *Three-Headed Alien*
- *Walk and Rename Objects*
- *What Are You Doing?*

# Appendix U

## Exercises to Strengthen Focus, Awareness, and Observation

- *Come Join Me*
- *Explosion Tag*
- *Freeze Tag*
- *Observe 6*
- *Simultaneous Clap*
- *Slow-Motion Tag*
- *Walk and Rename Objects*
- *Zing*

# Appendix V

*Exercises to Strengthen Listening and Being Present*

- *Dinner Party*
- *One-Word-at-a-Time Storytelling or Storytelling Chorus*
- *Simultaneous Clap*
- *Three-Headed Alien*
- *What Are You Doing?*
- *Zing*

# Appendix W

## *Exercises to Physically Energize*

- *Come Join Me*
- *Explosion Tag*
- *Kitty Wants a Corner*
- *Slow-Motion Tag*
- *Walk and Rename Objects*

# Bibliography

American Optometric Association. 2019. "New WHO Guidance: Very Limited Daily Screen Time Recommended for Children under 5." May 6, 2019. https://www.aoa.org.

Bonczek, Rose Burnett, and David Storck. 2012. *Ensemble Theatre Making: A Practical Guide*. London: Routledge.

Bonczek, Rose Burnett, Roger Manix, and David Storck. 2018. *Turn That Thing Off! Collaboration and Technology in 21C Actor Training*. London: Routledge.

Calderone, Marina, and Maggie Lloyd-Williams. 2004. *Actions: The Actors' Thesaurus*. London: Nick Hern Books.

Christakis, Erika, and Nicholas Christakis. 2010. "Want to Get Your Kids into College? Let Them Play." CNN, December 29, 2010. https://www.cnn.com.

Denworth, Lydia. 2019. "How Eye Contact Prepares the Brain to Connect." *Psychology Today*, February 25, 2019. https://www.psychologytoday.com.

Doucleff, Michaeleen, and Allison Aubrey. 2018. "Smartphone Detox: How to Power Down in a Wired World." NPR, February 12, 2018. https://www.npr.org.

Feiler, Bruce. 2015. "Hey, Kids, Look at Me When We're Talking." *New York Times*, April 17, 2015. https://www.nytimes.com.

Figueiro, M. G., Brittany Wood, Barbara Pliynick, and Mark S. Rea. 2011. "The Impact of Light from Computer Monitors on Melatonin Levels in College Students." *Neuro Endocrinology Letters* 32, no. 2. http://www.nel.edu/userfiles/articlesnew/NEL320211A03.pdf.

Forman, Milos, dir. *Hair*. United Artists Pictures, 1979. Film.

*Friends*. "The One with Ross's Wedding: Part 1." Episode 96. Directed by Kevin S. Bright. Written by Michael Borkow. NBC, May 7, 1998.

Geiger, Tray. 2018. "The Effects of Working Conditions on Teacher Retention." *Teachers and Teaching: Theory and Practice* 24, no. 6. https://www.tandfonline.com.

Gray, Peter. 2011. "The Decline of Play and the Rise of Psychopathology in Children and Adolescents." *The Strong: American Journal of Play* 3, no 4: 443–63. https://www.journalofplay.org.

Gregoire, Carolyn. 2013. "How Technology Is Killing Eye Contact." *Huffpost*, September https://www.huffpost.com.

Hagen, Uta, and Haskel Frankel. 1973. *Respect for Acting*. 2nd ed. New York: Macmillan.

Halpern, Charna, Del Close, and Kim "Howard" Johnson. 1994. *Truth in Comedy: The Manual of Improvisation*. Colorado Springs, CO: Meriwether Press.

Hayden, Erik. 2010. "Today's College Students Lacking in Empathy." *Pacific Standard*, May 31, 2010. Last updated June 14, 2017. https://psmag.com.

Hayes, Trevor. 2018. "Dopamine, Smartphones and You: A Battle for Your Time." *SITN* (blog), May 1, 2018. http://sitn.hms.harvard.edu/flash/2018/dopamine-smartphones-battle-time.

Hietanen, Jari K. 2018. "Affective Eye Contact: An Integrative Review." *Frontiers in Psychology*, August 28, 2018. https://www.frontiersin.org.

Johnstone, Keith. 2007. *Impro: Improvisation and the Theatre*. London: Routledge.

Lerman, Liz, and John Borstel. 2003. *Critical Response Process: A Method of Getting Useful Feedback on Anything You Make from Dance to Dessert*. Tacoma Park, MD: Liz Lerman Dance Exchange.

Madson, Patricia Ryan. 2005. *Improv Wisdom: Don't Prepare, Just Show Up*. New York: Bell Tower.

Mayo Clinic. n.d. "Fitness Basics." Accessed June 18, 2020. https://www.mayoclinic.org.

Reilly, Katie. 2017. "Is Recess Important for Kids or a Waste of Time? Here's What the Research Says." *Time*, October 23, 2017. https://time.com.

Rizga, Kristina. 2011. "What Standardized Tests Miss." *Mother Jones*, May 19, 2011. https://www.motherjones.com.

Rodenburg, Patsy. 2008. *The Second Circle: How to Use Positive Energy for Success in Every Situation*. New York: Norton.

Russo, Anthony, and Joe Russo, dirs. *Avengers: Infinity War*. Marvel Studios, 2018. Film002E.

Singer, Bryan, dir. 1995. *The Usual Suspects*. Polygram Filmed Entertainment, 1995. Film.

Stober, Dan. 2012. "Multitasking May Harm the Social and Emotional Development of Tweenage Girls, but Face-to-Face Talks Could Save the Day, Say Stanford Researchers." *Stanford News*, January 25, 2012. https://news.stanford.edu.

Supiano, Beckie. 2013. "More Students Turn to Social Media to Inform Their College Search." *Chronicle of Higher Education*, September 4, 2013. https://www.chronicle.com.

Szalavitz, Maia. 2010. "Shocker: Empathy Dropped 40% in College Students Since 2000." *Psychology Today*, May 28, 2010. https://www.psychologytoday.com.

Tyson, Neil deGrasse. 2008. "10 Questions for Neil deGrasse Tyson." *Time*, June 26, 2008. https://time.com.

Williams, Bronwyn T. 2005. "Standardized Students: The Problems with Writing for Tests Instead of People." *Journal of Adolescent and Adult Literacy* 49, no. 2. https://www.jstor.org.

# Index

acting, 1, 5, 11, 85, 105; adaptability, 53, 69, 77; audience relationship, 6, 11, 24, 50, 63, 103, 108; awareness, 22, 63; being present, 6; character, 9, 12, 20–21, 108, 111; commitment, 9, 24, 64, 65, 71, 75; empathy, 76; environment, 53, 59; definition of, 50; impulses, 4, 9, 69, 94; judgment, 63, 85, 105; listening, 6, 72, 76; objectives, 9, 18, 20; originality, 75; partners, 5, 12, 18, 21, 47, 64, 67, 69, 70, 71, 72, 76–77; process, xi, 1, 6, 11–12, 50, 53, 64, 111; research, 111; spontaneity, 64, 69; training, 2, 11–12, 26, 27, 45, 58–59, 63. *See also* actions; acting skills, teaching applications; collaboration; physical storytelling; rehearsal process; status; Yes And

acting skills, teaching applications, ix, x, 45–46, 62, 64; adaptability, 69, 91–92; awareness, 22, 54, 60, 61, 68, 92; being present, x, 6–7, 54, 68; commitment, 9, 18, 61, 64, 75, 76, 86, 87; Dare to Make the Obvious Choice, 70, 75–76, 107; flexibility, 51, 64, 69; Follow the Fear, 70, 73–75, 107; honesty, 51, 69, 69–70, 76, 94; listening, 6–7, 26, 55, 61, 67–68, 69, 72, 86, 88, 97; Make Your Partner Look Good, 70, 72–73, 107; observation, 8, 17, 56, 60, 68, 92, 154; sample lesson plan, application of acting skills, 28–30; spontaneity, 69, 120; Take Care of and Support Your Partner, 70, 72, 76–77, 107; vulnerability, 67, 73; Yes And, 6, 7, 54, 70, 71–72, 86, 102, 103, 107, 120, 122, 136, 146, 152. *See also* collaboration; collaborative learning; collaborative techniques; empathy; ensemble; exercises to develop/strengthen skills of; objectives; status; teacher, physical storytelling, vocal preparation; trust; Yes And

actions, 20–21, 107; beat, unit of action, 21; definition of, 20, 21; examples of, 20–21, 22–23, 29–30, 97; lesson plan, teaching applications, 21, 22–23, 29–30, 52, 97; passive actions, 21; writing, 107. *See also* As If; objectives; obstacles

*Actions: The Actors' Thesaurus*, 20, 21
Alda, Alan, 2
Ansell, Steve, 75
As If, 21
assessment (evaluation), 43–44; classroom environment, 50–51; course, 13–15; students, 23, 43–44, 73, 92; techniques, 43, 92; writing, 101–102, 107–108. *See also* teacher, self-assessment
audience, 34, 35, 36, 65, 117; expectations, 33, 48; reception, 1, 6, 11, 24, 108, 115. *See also* acting, audience relationship;

directing; students, as audience

*Blind Offers*, 55, 119–120, 181
Bonczek, Rose Burnett, 26, 84
Borstel, John, 109

Calderone, Marina, 20
Christakis, Erika, 3
Christakis, Nicholas, 3
classroom. *See* learning environment
Close, Del, 73
collaboration, 4, 66; actors, 64; confidence, 8; definition of, 8; expectations, 67; principles of, 67, 70–78; sacrifice, 8, 81; teaching, 8. *See also* collaborative learning; collaborative techniques; play, collaboration; storytelling, collaboration; theater, collaboration
collaborative learning, xix, 2, 5, 8, 41, 42, 46, 61, 67, 81, 86, 89, 93, 106, 115. *See also* collaborative techniques; ensemble; exercises to develop/strengthen skills of, collaboration; writing
collaborative techniques, x, xviii, 1, 5, 6, 7, 61, 67–69, 70–76, 83, 85, 102, 103, 106, 107. *See also* collaboration; collaborative learning
*Come Join Me*, 91, 121–123, 181, 183, 185, 189
comfort zone, 69. *See also* students, comfort zone; teacher, comfort zone
competition, 8; and students, xvii, 73, 75, 123. *See also* grading
conflict. *See* story, conflict; students, behavior
*Count to 20*, 61, 181
*Critical Response Process: A Method for Getting Useful Feedback on Anything from Dance to Dessert*, 109
course scheduling, 16–17; impact on teaching effectiveness, 16; time pressure, 19, 21, 25, 26, 45, 47, 71, 93
criticism. *See* students, constructive feedback

deGrasse Tyson, Neil, 14
De Matteo, Christian, 28, 66, 102

*The Decline of Play and the Rise of Psychopathology in Children and Adolescents*, 3
*Dinner Party*, 78, 87, 125–127, 179, 181, 187
directing, 79, 84, 91, 108; actors, 9, 36, 88, 103; audience, 84, 108; communication, 88, 96, 103–105; definition of responsibilities, 83, 84, 85, 86; environment, 50, 85; ego, 79; example of, 45–46; leadership, 83, 91; notes for actors, 39–40, 46, 94, 103; research, 110, 113. *See also* directing skills, teaching applications; plays (text)
directing skills, teaching applications, xix, 83, 84, 86; adaptability, 91; environment, 84, 99; Host of the Party, 84–86, 88; leadership, 81, 83, 84–85, 91, 99; Pass the ball, 85. *See also* directing; trust
director. *See* directing
discussion(s), 53; about challenges in a course/assignment, 20; classroom, 29, 44, 98, 112; collaboration, 6, 7, 72–73, 134, 135, 158; discussion techniques, 109; focus, xi; memory and retention, 142; about observations, 56; about reading assignments, 72–73, 76; structure, 21, 30; student participation, 40, 60, 69, 72–73, 80, 89, 136; student-teacher guidance discussions, 42, 74, 86, 94; teacher's prompts, 77, 80, 95, 109; about writing, 29, 102, 109, 114. *See also* imagination, class discussions; students, participation

empathy, x, 26, 67–68, 70, 76, 87, 97, 138, 142, 150, 163; decrease in college students, 2–3; smartphones, 68. *See also* exercises to develop/strengthen skills of, empathy
ensemble (team building), 77, 84, 117; challenges to, 97, 98; collaboration, 5; creating, 45–46, 67–69, 76, 84, 86; definition of, 67; elements of ensemble building, 68–69; leadership, 83, 84–86, 91, 92, 99. *See also* exercises to develop/strengthen skills of, ensemble

*Ensemble Theatre Making: A Practical Guide*, 77, 84
environment, 85; impact of physical surroundings on teaching, 17–18, 49, 50, 51, 57, 58; less than ideal conditions in classroom, 56, 58–59; lesson plan, using physical surroundings for, 53; transforming attitudes towards physical surroundings, 50–51, 57–59, 60–61, 153–155. *See also* learning environment
evaluation. *See* assessment (evaluation)
exercises to develop/strengthen skills of: awareness, 129–131, 137–139, 141–142, 149–150, 161–163; being open and receptive, 161–163; collaboration, 58–62, 78, 86–88, 119–120, 121–123, 125–127, 133–136, 145–147, 149–150, 151–152, 161–163, 181; commitment, 121–123, 133–136, 137–139, 153–155, 157–158; communication, 119–120, 133–136, 137–139, 157–158, 161–163; concentration, 125–127, 149–150; confidence, 119–120, 133–136, 137–139, 141–143, 153–155, 157–158, 165–167; empathy, 125–127, 137–139, 141–143, 149–150, 161–163; ensemble building, 121–123, 125–127, 145–147, 161–163; eye contact, 125–127, 137–139, 141–143, 149–150, 161–163; focus, 125–127, 141–142, 145–147, 149–150, 151–152, 153–155, 161–163, 185; honesty, 149–150; icebreakers, 179; imagination, 59–61, 121–123, 133–136, 153–155, 157–158, 183; listening and being present, 125–127, 137–139, 145–147, 149–150, 151–152, 157–158, 161–163, 187; memory and retention, 125–127, 141–143, 153–155; observation skills, 119–120, 141–143, 153–155, 185; physically energize, 137–139, 153–155, 189; risk taking, 133–136, 137–139; stamina, 129–131, 137–139, 157–158; specificity, 121–123, 133–136; spontaneity, 129–131, 151–152, 157–158; storytelling, 47, 145–147, 151–152; strategic thinking, 125–127, 129–131; taking care of partners, 125–127, 151–152; trust, 119–120, 137–139, 145–147, 161–163; vulnerability, 137–139, 141–143; Yes And, 119–120, 121–123, 145–147, 151–152. *See also* writing, exercises

*Explosion Tag*, 88, 129–131, 185, 189
eye contact, 30, 78; empathy, 68; and smartphones, 68; and students, 53, 68, 79, 80, 87, 126, 127, 138, 150, 162, 163. *See also* empathy; exercises to develop/strengthen skills of, empathy

failure, 40; accepting, 44, 61, 94, 138, 139; fear of, 3, 4, 67, 74, 112; learning from, 40–42, 44, 45, 61, 66, 67, 74, 88, 89, 94, 106; overcoming failure, 40, 44–45, 61, 73–74, 94; in rehearsals, 40, 88; students, 4, 41, 44, 66, 67, 89, 105, 106, 112, 138, 139. *See also* acting skills, teaching applications, Follow the Fear; teacher, failure
falling action. *See* story, falling action
fear, 4; of being wrong, 4, 42, 60, 74, 146, 154; and confidence, 4, 9, 60, 74, 112–113; of judgment, 3, 60, 74, 110, 120, 130, 146, 152; learning environment, 3, 5, 9, 136; overcoming fear, 4, 5, 9, 55, 62, 73–75, 103, 112–113, 115; of performance, 42; power of, 74, 110; of rejection, 3, 42, 60, 74, 120, 130, 139; role of fear in learning, 74; and students, 4, 5, 42, 54, 60, 73–75, 110, 112, 113, 114, 115, 136; and teacher, 4, 20, 63. *See also* acting skills, teaching applications, Follow the Fear; failure, fear of; play, fear
*Freeze Tag*, 87, 133–136, 183, 185, 189; *No Question Freeze Tag*, 134; *Three-Word Freeze Tag*, 134
*Friends*, 57

games, 3, 86; for assessment of students, 16, 92, 98; eye contact, 87; as icebreakers, 86; imagination, 3; *Jeopardy*, variations for the classroom, 47, 51, 92, 93, 134; physical games, 87, 88; in place of test/quiz, 92; to restore

collaborative connections, 91; role of games in learning, 2, 47, 69, 80, 85, 87, 93; story games, 47; student-designed, 16, 47, 92, 98. *See also* exercises to develop/strengthen skills of
gesture, 24, 79, 146. *See also* teacher, gesture
goals. *See* objectives
grading, xvii, xix, 23, 40, 44, 67, 73, 89, 90, 94, 114
Gray, Peter, 3

Hagen, Uta, 177
*Hair*, 14
Hero's Journey, 35–36; obstacles to, 40–42; student assignment, 37, 38–39, 42
homework, 42, 72, 79, 88–90, 92, 93, 154
Hopkins, Melanie, 65

imagination, 3, 4, 38, 53, 74; class discussions, 8; play, 3, 7; role in learning, 7–8, 18, 53, 60, 74, 102; story, 2, 51; and students, 7–8, 34, 60; and teacher, 7, 8, 9, 21, 38, 52, 57. *See also* acting
*Impro*, 22, 55, 75, 119–120
*Improv Wisdom*, 74
improvisation, 47, 58–59, 73, 74, 76, 77; applied, 2, 51, 89; definition of, 53; Take Care of and Support Your Partner, 76. *See also* acting skills, teaching applications; Yes And
inciting incident. *See* story, inciting incident

Johnstone, Keith, 22, 55–56, 59–61, 75, 79, 119–120, 153–155
Jones, Dr. Carleton, 174

*Kitty Wants a Corner*, 137–139, 179, 189

Laban Movement Analysis, 51–52, 169–170
learning environment, 9, 90, 97, 99; activating learning environment, 54; behavior, 97–98; confidence, 9; exercises to transform physical and psychological environment, 53–56; expectations, 34, 36, 49, 66, 67, 85, 107, 111, 112; safe space, 67, 97, 99; shared space, xviii, xix, 49–50, 53, 61, 62; transforming learning environment, 53, 59; trust, 5, 9, 45, 90, 97, 99. *See also* environment; failure; fear; students, participation; Us vs. Them
lecture, 17, 36, 38; attention span, 62; changing traditional lecture, 8, 45, 53; storytelling techniques, 34, 45, 53; structure, 21, 30, 36; student responses to, xi, 7, 35, 40, 53; teacher preparation, xi, 21, 27, 30, 31, 34–35, 38, 39, 52
Lerman, Liz, 109
lesson plans, 28–31, 34, 37, 38–39, 41–42; applying Personal Analysis to sample lesson plan, 28–31; physical movement, 52; research, 37; as story, xviii, 13–15, 34, 35, 36–39, 41–42, 47–48, 50. *See also* actions, lesson plan, teaching applications; lesson plan samples for
lesson plan samples for: biology, 89; english, 41, 53, 101; history, 7, 23, 37, 41, 93; math, 22, 37, 46; political science, 23, 134; psychology, 89, 111, 112; science, 2, 74; speech, 23, 43, 66, 94; writing, 28–30, 41, 74, 102
listening. *See* acting skills, teaching applications, listening; exercises to develop/strengthen skills of, listening
Lloyd-Williams, Maggie, 20–21

Make Your Partner Look Good. *See* acting skills, teaching applications
Manix, Roger, 26
Maslow's Hierarchy of Needs, 89
May, Marlene, 65
mistakes, 42, 65

Nickerson, Jay, 65
No, But response, 86, 88; definition of, 71
notes, 34, 40, 43; methods of taking notes, 39–40, 94; retention and absorption, 6, 40; role of notes in learning, 40, 106. *See also* directing, notes for actors

objectives, 44, 58; active (positive) objectives, 19; creating, 8–9, 16, 24, 37–38; definition of, 16, 177; examples of, 18, 22; methods of achieving, 9, 16, 20, 21, 22–23, 36, 39, 58; passive (negative) objectives, 18–19; raising the stakes (level of importance), 23. *See also* acting, objectives; obstacles

*Observe 6*, 68, 141–143, 179, 185

observation. *See* acting skills, teaching applications

obstacles, 19; in the classroom, 19, 92; environment, 53; methods of overcoming, 19–20

*One-Word-at-a-Time Storytelling*, 47, 145–147

*Pass the Story*, 75

Permission to Screw Up, 41–42, 104, 105–106

*Physical Exercise: Home Rehearsal for Teachers*, 165–167

physical preparation. *See* teacher, physical preparation

physical storytelling, 24. *See also* teacher, physical storytelling

play, 1, 3; benefits of, 2, 4, 5, 47; children, 3, 4; collaboration, 1, 2, 4, 5, 85; desire to play, 3; effects of too little play time, 2–3; fear, 3, 4, 5; introducing play in classroom, 3, 5, 47, 88, 93; peer pressure, 3; playing actions, 21, 22, 22–23, 52; research, 2; role of play in emotional development, 2, 3; role of play in learning, xi, 1, 2–3, 8; societal expectations, 3; theater as play, 2, 3, 7. *See also* acting, character; collaboration; *The Decline of Play and the Rise of Psychopathology in Children and Adolescents*; imagination; status

plays (text), 39–40, 64, 93, 108, 110; directing, 84, 113; world of the play, xix, 2, 50, 83, 113; writing a play, class assignment, 74

*Please/No*, 133

rehearsal process, 5, 6, 9, 39, 46, 47, 53, 84, 85, 86, 88, 96, 97, 103–104, 105, 108

retention of information, xviii, 26, 95, 125–127. *See also* exercises to develop/ strengthen skills of, memory and retention

retention rates, xii

risk taking. *See* students, risk taking; teaching, risk taking

Ryan Madson, Patricia, 74

Shakespeare, William, ix, 15–16

*Simultaneous Clap*, 149–150, 179, 185, 187

sleep, 26; effects on teaching, 26; methods to encourage, 26. *See also* smartphones, sleep

*Slow-Motion Tag*, 87, 183, 185, 189

smartphones, 26, 68; dopamine release, 26; eye contact, 68, 126, 163; focus, 20; impact on collaborative behaviors, 26; impact on memory and retention, 127; policy for use in classroom, 18, 20, 30, 163; sleep, 26; student's relationship to, 18, 20, 26, 54, 126, 163. *See also* empathy; technology; *Turn That Thing Off! Collaboration and Technology in 21st-Century Actor Training*

speech classes, 23, 43, 66, 94

Spolin, Viola, 121–123

status (hierarchy of power), 22–23, 78–80; changing status, 78–79; and confidence, 79, 80; definition of, 22, 78, 80; environment, 22; examples of high status, 23, 79, 80, 97; examples of loss of status, 79; examples of low status, 22, 78, 79, 80; hierarchy, 22, 78, 81; leadership, 83; methods of establishing, 79, 80–81; physical expression of, 78; preferred status, 78

*Stop/Go*, 87

Storck, David, 26, 69, 77, 84

story, xi, xviii, 33; application in classroom, 13–15, 28, 34, 37–39, 41–42, 71; arc, 21, 36; climax, 13, 35, 43–44; conflict, 133, 134, 136; cultural references, 14–15, 37; environment, 48, 49, 51; falling action, 35, 44; impact on audience, 1, 11, 33–34, 35, 36, 38, 63; inciting incident, 35, 36–38, 41, 42; structure, 12, 34–36, 64, 71, 105, 114; teaching applications, xii, 8, 11; why story is needed, 14, 14–15. *See also*

# Index

games, story games; Hero's Journey; imagination, story; lesson plan, as story; storytelling

storytelling, 6, 24, 47, 49, 50, 122; collaboration, 4, 11, 41, 42, 46, 50, 64, 71, 72, 75, 99; confidence, 45; environment, 49, 51; examples in the classroom, 13–14, 28, 43, 44, 75; physical storytelling, 24. *See also* acting; exercises to develop/strengthen skills of, storytelling; learning environment; lecture; students, as performers; teacher, physical storytelling

*Storytelling Chorus*, 47, 146–147, 187

students: accountability, 13, 89, 90; as acting partners to teachers, x, xix, 53, 63, 64–66, 67, 70, 72–73, 78, 83, 107; agency, 36, 39, 42, 47, 92, 109, 113, 114; anxiety, 3, 20, 86, 105, 111, 161; as audience, 36, 62, 63–64; awareness, 3, 26, 28, 54, 60, 61, 68, 120, 130, 135, 138, 150, 154; behavior, xi, xii, 8, 56, 67, 96–98, 136; being present, 6, 54, 56, 60, 68; boredom, xviii, 18, 76, 113; career preparation, x, 8, 9, 28, 29, 30, 42, 84, 102–103, 115, 117; college readiness, 2–3, 104; comfort zone, 9, 45, 54, 135; commitment, 61; communication, 6, 16, 28, 29, 30, 55, 102, 103, 134, 135, 138, 139; concentration, 20, 87, 88, 142, 147; confidence, 5, 7, 8, 9, 21, 22–23, 39, 50, 72, 73, 92, 94, 112, 120, 154, 158; constructive feedback, 72, 107–108, 109, 110; curiosity, 36, 60; disciplining, 96–98; economic inequities, xviii; engagement, 35, 36, 38–39, 47, 50, 51, 62, 84; focus, xi, xii, 35, 39, 54, 56, 60, 87; impact of a course's scheduled time on learning, 16–17; impulses, 7, 9, 54, 55, 62, 69, 85–86, 105; listening, 6, 7, 26, 36, 55, 72, 146, 158; memory and retention, xviii, 26, 40, 126; motivating, 36–38; originality, 75–76; ownership of learning skills, 9, 44, 72, 73, 111, 114; participation, 20, 55, 67, 80, 86, 89, 120, 130, 135; as performers (storytellers), xix, 42, 43, 44, 111–112; potential, xix, 38, 139; preparedness, xviii, 68, 88, 89–90, 101, 102; reading comprehension, 95; research, 110, 111–112, 113, 114; risk taking, 5, 8, 45, 50, 73, 74, 75, 76, 85, 99, 106, 135; student loan debt, xviii, 58; study habits, xi, 94; taking responsibility, 13, 77, 88, 90, 135, 163; tuition, 2, 58, 59, 92, 94. *See also* assessment (evaluation); collaborative learning; competition; discussion; empathy; environment; failure; fear; grading; imagination, and students; learning environment; play; smartphones; trust, students; writing

student/teacher relationship, xii, xiii, 5, 63, 92. *See also* Us vs. Them

tactics, 38, 42, 79. *See also* actions

teacher, 78, 83, 85–86; adaptability, 13, 91–92; awareness, 31, 51, 68, 79, 92, 165; comfort zone, 24; confidence, 4, 15, 23, 24, 51, 52, 76, 88; ego, 66, 76, 78, 83; empathy, xi, 67–68, 165; failure, 45, 66, 76; gesture, 13, 24, 51, 79, 166, 169–170; honesty, 69–70; humor, 13, 18, 28, 40, 80, 86; impact of course scheduling, 16–17; intuition, xviii, 68; leadership, 83–85, 91, 94, 99; listening, 7; passion for teaching, xvii, xix, 8, 12; as performer, x–xi, xviii–xix, 1, 11, 12–13, 15–16, 16, 28, 30–31, 34, 35, 36, 45, 63, 64, 68, 99; Personal Analysis, 12–24, 28–30, 37, 65; personal goals, xvii, 16, 23, 29, 37; personal process, 11, 12, 31; personal relationship to course material, 15–16; personal strengths, 13; physical preparation, 24–25, 30, 51; physical storytelling, 24, 51–52; respect, 20, 57, 58, 67, 98; risk taking, 76; self-assessment, 11, 12–13, 24, 51; self-care, 25–26, 27, 65–66; self-empowerment, 19, 57; self-trust, 45, 99; speech, 27, 173; stamina, 25, 69; stress, 20, 25, 171; vocal preparation, 27, 31; *Vocal Warm Up*, 171–174; vulnerability, 67. *See also* ensemble, creating; fear, and teacher; imagination,

Index 199

and teacher; *Physical Exercise: Home Rehearsal for Teachers*
teacher/student relationship. *See* student/teacher relationship
teaching: adapting theater concepts to classroom, ix, x, xviii, 11, 22–23, 68–69, 101; administration, relationship to, 91; attrition rates, 57; commitment, 86; morale, xvii, 56–59; resources, xviii; skills, ix, xi, 5, 9, 31, 34, 62; unexpected challenges, 91. *See also* acting skills, teaching applications; directing skills, teaching applications; environment, impact of physical surroundings on teaching; notes; objectives, creating; trust, establishing; writing
team building. *See* ensemble
technology, xii, 102; in the classroom, 2, 26, 92; college readiness, 2; impact of excessive use on collaborative skills, 26; screen time, 26, 87, 138, 163; writing, 28. *See also* smartphones; *Turn That Thing Off! Collaboration and Technology in 21st-Century Actor Training*
*Temples of Stone: Exploring the Megalithic Tombs of Ireland*, 174
testing, 43, 92, 94, 101
textbooks, 94–95
theater, 1, 117; audience, 1; benefits of, 4; collaboration, xviii, 2, 4–5, 8; definition of, x, xvii–xviii, 1; fear, 4; imagination, 7; relationship to teaching, ix–xi, 1; training, 2, 11. *See also* acting, training; acting skills, teaching applications; competition; play; plays (text); storytelling; theater skills
theater games. *See* exercises to develop/strengthen skills of
theater skills, ix, 4–5, 6, 7, 8, 70; definition of, 5. *See also* acting skills, teaching applications; collaboration; directing skills, teaching applications; theater
*Three-Headed Alien*, 47, 86, 92, 151–152, 181, 183, 187
trust, 5; acting, 5; breaking trust, 88, 90, 94, 103; directing, 84, 99; ensemble, 94; establishing, 4–5, 7, 9, 54, 55, 90,
97; students, 45, 54, 62, 99, 138, 163. *See also* exercises to develop/strengthen skills of, trust; learning environment; teacher, self-trust
Turkle, Dr. Sherry, 26
*Turn That Thing Off! Collaboration and Technology in 21st-Century Actor Training*, 26

Us vs. Them, xvii, xviii, xix, 5, 8, 9, 36, 49, 63
*The Usual Suspects*, 78–79

*Vocal Warm Up*, 171–174. *See also* teacher, vocal preparation
voice. *See* teacher: vocal preparation

*Walk and Rename Objects*, 59–61, 87, 153–155, 183, 185, 189
*What Are You Doing?*, 54–55, 87, 91, 157–158, 179, 183, 187
writing, 102, 110; assignments, 15, 29–30, 43, 74, 107, 111; collaborative learning, 102, 107–110, 115; communication, 102; confidence, 110, 112; constructive feedback, 106–109, 110, 114; courses, 15, 43, 74, 101, 102, 104, 109; cover letters, 28, 29, 30, 102, 115; drafts, 41, 102, 103, 104, 105, 106, 107, 108, 109–110, 114; exercises, 30, 75; essays, 37, 38–39, 41, 43, 104, 105, 106, 108; free-writes, 75; outlines, 9, 41, 95, 105–106; personal investment in, 111–112, 113–114; plays and scenes, 74, 89; process of, 102, 105–106, 110, 115; as a requirement, 101; research, 102, 108, 110, 111–112, 113–114; revision process, 105–106, 108, 109–110; skills, 16, 28, 29, 30, 37, 75, 101, 102, 110, 115; standardized tests, 101; story, 38–39, 111; student preparedness, 101–102; teaching, 38–39, 40, 101–103, 104, 105–106, 107–110; theater techniques applied to, 101, 102, 103, 105–106, 107–108, 111, 115; thesis, 37, 38, 39, 95, 105, 108, 111, 112, 113, 114, 134; workshops, 107–108, 109. *See also* assessment (evaluation); lesson plan samples for,

writing

Yes And, 6; acting, 6; definition of, 6; improvisation, 6, 71, 76, 103. *See also* acting; acting skills, teaching

applications, Yes And; exercises to develop/strengthen skills of, Yes And

*Zing*, 53–54, 87, 91, 161–163, 179, 185, 187

# About the Authors

**Michael Flanagan** is a theater director and Instructor of Drama at Houston Community College. He is associate producer of Gi60 Live US Edition, the international one-minute play festival where, over the years, he's directed over 100 short plays. Flanagan has taught theater and directed for colleges and universities such as The College of Mount Saint Vincent, Brooklyn College, Iona College, and Fordham University. He has directed productions Off-off Broadway, for community theaters and at theatre festivals, as well as adjudicating performing arts competitions. He was the founding artistic director for the Roosevelt Island Shakespeare Festival and assisted in the development of The City Island Theatre Shakespeare Festival. As Assistant Director of Student Success and Assistant Chair of General Education at The College of Westchester, he used applied theater concepts and techniques to develop the curriculum of freshman seminar and other core curriculum classes. He also applied improvisation and theatrical concepts to the Student Success Coach Program. He holds an MFA in Theatre Directing from Brooklyn College.

**Rose Burnett Bonczek** is a theater educator, director, and author with over 40 years of experience in the field. She is the recipient of the 2018 Oscar Brockett Outstanding Teacher of Theatre in Higher Education award from the Association for Theater in Higher Education and recipient of the 2018 Excellence in Creative Achievement from Brooklyn College, City University of New York. She is the coauthor of *Turn That Thing Off! Collaboration and Technology in 21C Actor Training* with Roger Manix and David Storck, *Ensemble Theatre Making: A Practical Guide* with David Storck, and *One Minute Plays: A Practical Guide to Tiny Theatre* with Steve Ansel. She has taught acting, improvisation, directing, and methods of collaboration and was director of the BFA Acting program at Brooklyn College, City University of New York for over 20 years. Currently, she teaches and coaches privately and works as a consultant for organizations such as Atlantic Theatre Company, the Theater Association of New York State, and Stable Cable Lab Company. Bonczek is artistic director of the US Edition of Gi60 (Gone in 60 Seconds): International One Minute Theatre Festival – http://gi60.blogspot.com. Gi60's YouTube Channel features over 1,500 one minute plays performed over the past 16 years: www.youtube.com/user/gi60channel. Bonczek has directed over 100 productions Off and Off-off Broadway, for regional and community theaters, at international festivals, and in educational environments.

www.ingramcontent.com/pod-product-compliance
Lightning Source LLC
Chambersburg PA
CBHW030137240426
43672CB00005B/164